WE
JEWS

WE JEWS

Invitation to a Dialogue

EFRAIM M. ROSENZWEIG

Illustrations by Mary Ann Scherr

HAWTHORN BOOKS, INC.
Publishers/NEW YORK

) Judaism

1) practices
2) interaction with others

WE JEWS

Library of Congress Catalog Card Number: 77-81359
ISBN: 0-8015-8428-0
 2 3 4 5 6 7 8 9 10

Dedicated
to
our children and our children's children
and
to yours

CONTENTS

FOREWORD

The purpose of this guide is to present the Jew "whole," as it were. It was not my intention to present a heavily documented study. On the contrary, from the outset I had in mind a sort of a *vade mecum*, an easily read handbook that the average person could read within a few hours.

Obviously, such a text cannot be all inclusive; a vast amount of material had to be omitted, and much of what was included had to be substantially simplified. Still, it was felt desirable to include discussion of subjects to which the Christian reader might have been exposed and that might have piqued his curiosity. To that end, topics found in the chapter on "Some Bypaths" were included. At all times, I have been guided by the desire to provide answers to questions put to me over the years.

It is my hope that the reader will be stimulated to turn to books that offer a more detailed study of special areas of interest. But, even without such additional reading, the reader should be able to gain an overall view of the principal forces and factors that were operative in the making of the modern Jew, and will derive a reasonably clear understanding of what Jewish life is like in its many aspects.

Every effort has been made to present a balanced and objective description of traditions other than my own. I am indebted to my friend and colleague, Dr. Simha Kling, who was kind enough to offer a number of valuable suggestions. I am also indebted to the numerous participants in Christian discussion groups and classes that I addressed over the years of my rabbinate, not the least among which have been my classes at the Southeastern Baptist Theological Seminary. I have learned from all of them.

I am, finally, deeply indebted to George Scheer, without whose encouragement the writing of this guide would not have been undertaken, and whose critical reading of the text in its various stages of development was creatively and helpfully perceptive.

EFRAIM M. ROSENZWEIG

INTRODUCTION

> . . . lo, *a people living by themselves, not accounting themselves as one of the nations.*
> *The Complete Bible*, an American translation

> . . . lo, *the people shall dwell alone, and shall not be reckoned among the nations.*
> King James Version

These two translations of Numbers 23:9 are part of a statement made by Balaam, a soothsayer from Pethor on the Euphrates. He had been called by Balak, King of Moab, to curse the Israelites, who were encamped in the Jordan Valley. The statement is quite compelling since it is prophetic of virtually all later Jewish history. Although derived from the identical biblical text, each of the above translations offers a different approach to Jewish "otherness." The first speaks of a self-chosen separateness, the second of a condition imposed from without.

In his statement, Balaam is referring to that grouping of Israelite tribes led by Moses, which was at that time in the process of finding its cohesive identity under the aegis of

their God, known to them by various names, but principally YHWH and Elohim. YHWH, referred to in Jewish
tradition as *Adonai* (Lord), had entered into covenant
with the Children of Israel at Sinai. Under the terms of the
covenant/treaty, the Israelites were to obey his laws and
statutes, and he would watch over their destiny. His intention with respect to the Children of Israel had already been
stated in his promise to Abram (Gen. 12:2), but now the
conditions of the covenanted selection were made clear.
The people gave assent: "All that the Lord has spoken, we
shall do" (Exod. 19:2), and from that time forward, the
people became the People. Faith and folk were inseparably
bound together. During the millennia that followed, we
became increasingly "other," apart.

As time went on, reaching into the Christian centuries,
because of our status as a religious minority in predominantly Christian cultures, our "otherness" engendered at
one end of the spectrum a mélange of myths and legends,
many of them hostile and dangerous, and, at the other, a
considerable amount of honest curiosity about Jewish
practices, beliefs, and community structure. For some of
the latter there are parallels in the Christian religious experience. But there is no parallel in the Christian's experience
to help him to understand fully Jewish peoplehood. All the
more, then, has there been difficulty in comprehending the
interfabricated nature of Jewish faith and folk.

How can the average non-Jew know how the Jew sees
himself? How can he know what forces and factors con-
tributed toward the shaping of the contemporary Jew?
There are very few non-Jews who search out the what,
how, and why of Jewish life and thought, just as there are
few Jews who do as much with respect to Christianity. On
the other hand, while there is an almost total exposure to

the many facets of the Christian religious culture, there is little comparable opportunity to see, hear, or read about the substance and core concerns of the Jewish life-style.

True, the Jew is known to a certain extent. Our festivals and holy days are often publicized in the mass media, and of course the State of Israel has been a frequent source of news. But I suspect that most Christians—apart from scholars—who have a serious or passing interest in the subject know the Jew, or know of the Jew, only through Sunday school texts, missionary tracts, or denominational publications. That such inquiry should be made at all is natural, for a faith that has historically regarded itself as "covenant successor" to the people of Israel, and the central figure of whose worship was himself a Jew, must inevitably try to have at least some understanding, however incomplete, of its Jewish roots.

But he who knows the Jew only from such sources of information can scarcely learn therefrom that between Bible times and the current day there has been an intervening period of great change in the development of Judaism, critical to an understanding of the modern Jew. We of today are products of yesterdays that did not come to an end when Jesus died on the cross.

Of what value is a more comprehensive understanding of Judaism and the Jew? Quite apart from providing a response to natural curiosity, it can be of deeper importance to the Christian: He can grasp with greater precision those facts and concepts that explain why the Jew has been for so long a "conscientious rejector" of beliefs so precious to Christianity.

However, it is the intention of this guide to go well beyond the what and the why of our religious beliefs and our festivals. There is the Jewish sanctuary and the Jewish home; there is the Jewish community; and there is the Jewish preoccupation with Israel. There is much to describe and to explain. There is nothing to conceal.

If I can succeed in my purposes, then this guide should be helpful in illuminating our common heritage, while at the same time the contours of historical and unbridgeable differences will be correctly defined.

It is my hope that what I have written will make some small contribution toward bringing more closely together in harmonious understanding strangers, neighbors, and friends.

WE
JEWS

1
WHO AND WHAT
WE ARE—
AND ARE NOT

i

First and foremost, it must not be assumed that all Jews are, as it were, cut from the same bolt of cloth. Jews are of all kinds and dispositions, of many different religious philosophies, holding a wide spectrum of attitudes with respect to all sorts of questions, problems, and issues. We are a quite diverse people, with what appears to be a built-in individualism. Moses complained to God that the Israelites were a "stiff-necked people," independent and unwilling to follow the leader, so to speak.

In saying that we are of many different religious philosophies, it should be clearly understood that such philosophies are all within the framework of a basic monotheism. The essential differences between Jewish religious groupings will be dealt with later. The point here is that there must be no inference that diverse religious philosophies include adherence to, or acceptance of, faiths other than the historically Jewish.

It is also important to understand that when there are

questions relating to the Jew, we are not dealing with faith alone. In the Introduction to this book, there is reference to "faith and folk." It may be useful and interesting to put the following question to the Christian reader: "What if you were no longer a "CHRISTian?" That is, what if you no longer believed in the basic tenets of Christian theology: i.e. the Trinity, Jesus as God's only begotten Son, the redemptive purpose of his death on the cross, his resurrection, and his second coming? If, in these historic terms, you were no longer a CHRISTian, a believer in Jesus as the Christ, what would you be? Some have referred to such non-CHRISTians as "Gentiles," "cultural Christians," or "sentimental Christians." Whatever designation is applicable, it is clear that individuals who have disassociated themselves from traditional or historic Christianity are not, nonetheless, de facto members of a "Christian folk." There is no ethnicity, no historic collectivity within which they can have identity as Christians.

Jews are not confronted by this problem. A Jew may accept in its totality all that Jewish theology has to say about God and man, or he may reject in whole or in part such theological tradition and teaching, and in ritual practice consider himself nonreligious, and yet, in terms of his ethnic or folk identity be a Jew. A nonreligious Jew, to be sure, but a Jew nonetheless. In short, whether a Jew is religious or secular in his orientation, he is still a Jew.

Having tried to give some hint of the varieties of shadings of Jewishness, it should prove helpful to narrow down the focus, the field of vision, so to speak. If there are religious and secular Jews, the following questions are in order: How is Jewish identity determined? And precisely what is a Jew? Can an individual simply declare himself to be a Jew? Can he be a Christian at the same time? Can he claim Jewish folk or ethnic identity, but follow a different faith?

As to Jewish identity: Anyone born of a Jewish mother, or who has been converted to the Jewish faith, is considered a Jew. The first part of this definition is simple enough. According to Jewish law, the child's faith follows the mother's. A child born to the unconverted wife of a Jew is not Jewish. While the male child born to a Jewish mother (herself born of a Jewish mother or converted to Judaism prior to his birth) is a Jew, it is required by Jewish law that he be circumcised eight days after his birth, unless there is a compelling medical reason why this cannot be done. The circumcision is a ritual act carried out by a skilled functionary called a mohel (circumciser), in the presence of at least ten males above the age of thirteen, who constitute a quorum.

A simple self-declaration is not a passport to Jewish identity. There have been non-Jews since ancient times who have been attracted to the Jewish faith, and who have shared in acts or Jewish worship (see Isa. 56:6). Whatever may have been their status of identity in Bible times, in our day such an act of sharing in worship or even of participation in Jewish communal life does not confer "Jewishness" upon such individuals. What is lacking is the formal act of conversion.

Just what should be required of a candidate for conversion is moot at the time of this writing. In fact, it has been the subject of heated debate. The reasons for the dispute is that traditional and liberal Jews often have radically different points of view about requirements for conversion: What must be learned, circumcision of the male convert, and ritual immersion are most extensively at issue. As a result, one sector of the Jewish community may accept a conversion as bona fide if it has been carried out by a Conservative or Reform rabbi, while another sector may not so accept it. Whatever resolution to this problem may come about in the near or remote future, it can be noted here, in response to the question "who is a Jew?" that a non-Jew can acquire Jewish identity through conversion.

Clearly, a non-Jew cannot become a Jew through simple self-declaration, any more than a newcomer to the United States can become a citizen without passing certain tests and, subsequent thereto, being duly sworn in. Unless there are established agreements, the citizen of one country cannot automatically become a citizen of another, thus enjoying the status of dual citizenship. In like manner, a Jew who has converted to Christianity cannot claim to be a "Jewish Christian" or a "Christian Jew." Such designations are so mutually contradictory as to be completely beyond serious consideration. There are nations that permit the status of dual citizenship with other states, but faiths such as Judaism and Christianity are, in terms of their respective theologies, too mutually exclusive to make such "dual citizenship" possible.

A Jew who has converted to Christianity cannot correctly refer to himself in hyphenated terms such as "Hebrew-Christian." To do so carries with it the suspicion of ulterior purpose, usually the intention to missionize. Uninformed Christians may find such a person wholly credible in his claims and self-evaluation, but to the Jew he lacks the authority of logic and common sense.

Somewhat related to this question is that of the individual who claims Jewish folk or ethnic identity but follows a different faith. Obviously, a person who has been brought up as a Jew may continue to carry within himself a knowledge of Jewish folk values, community institutions, and the like. But by giving up Judaism in favor of Christianity or any other faith, he has thereby also surrendered his right to speak in terms of his Jewish identity in any realistic way. For Jewish faith and folk are too closely interwoven to be that simply unraveled. There are a great many non-Jews who emphatically identify with Jewish concerns and values, but they do not identify themselves as Jews. The former Jew who is now a Christian cannot claim Jewish folk or ethnic *identity*: At best, he can speak of folk origins and previous folk or ethnic experience with understanding. The key to this position is that central to authentic Jewish identity is the commitment to the survival of the Jewish people, and from this writer's point of view, meaningful survival cannot be effected through any act, personal or collective, that separates faith from folk. Thus, to conclude, Judaism is the faith of the Jewish people. There are Jews whose religious devoutness is weak to the point of being virtually nonexistent. They define their nonreligiosity in terms that range all the way from nonobservance of traditional religious ritual through rejection of structured worship to outright atheism—although within my personal experience the latter are very few in number. These self-designated "secular" Jews, or "ethnic" Jews, are still Jews. However they define their Jewishness, there is still the core determination to be a Jew, to be known as a Jew, to support Jewish causes, and, in their chosen way, to play a part in the meaningful survival of the Jewish people.

ii

So much, then, for the question "who is a Jew?" The other question, *"what* is a Jew?" is quite different. We have been referred to as race, nation, religious community, people, and just "religion" unencumbered by "community." Can there be found and agreed upon one designation by which we can be characterized, and which will encompass the many facets of our diversity as faith and folk?

The least applicable, surely, is race, since, by definition, race is "a division of mankind possessing traits that are transmissible by descent and sufficient to characterize it as a distinct human type." There are simply no racial characteristics that all Jews share in common: skin pigmentation, hair types, physical features, and the like. There are fair-skinned Jews and dark, large-boned and slight of build, with straight nose and curved. It would be very difficult, to the point of impossible, to find common racial characteristics among Jews of Eastern and Western Europe, India, North Africa, the United States, and Israel. Whatever may have been the distinguishing characteristics of our ancestors from the days of Abraham, that "wandering Aramean," onward, the vagaries of our history have long since blurred them. No, we Jews are not a race.

Are we then a nation? A nation is defined as a community of people possessing a more or less defined territory and government. Save for the Jews who live in the State of Israel, there are none who, as Jews, possess either territory or government and are recognizable as national entities. Taken collectively, we are not a nation.

There are some Jews, minuscule in number, who deny the peoplehood, ethnicity, or other folk description of Jews, and who prefer to see us as a religion alone. Thus, for them, we Jews in the United States are "Americans of the Jewish faith." While such designation is true, it is incomplete since it ignores other formative phenomena of our millennia-long history.

Dr. Mordecai Kaplan, founder of the Reconstructionist movement, has persuasively argued that the Jewish collectivity is best designated as an "evolving religious civilization," a description he finds most suitable to bind together the faith and folk factors in Jewish life and history. There is no doubt that his thoughts on Judaism as civilization have had wide acceptance among Rabbis and other Jewish leaders. The evidence of our religious doctrines, coupled with laws, norms, agencies, and social institutions that have grown out of them since ancient times, justifies his use of the word *civilization*. Jewish faith and folk, therefore, thanks to characteristic ways of maintaining our collective identity and coping with the variety of life confrontations to which we have been exposed both individually and collectively, are the two major ingredients in the evolving Jewish religious civilization. That it is described as evolving points to a creatively adaptive future.

With all that, it is safe to say that the average Jew is not troubled by these questions and problems. He will probably say, "Whatever I am, I am. But whatever I am, I am a Jew." For my part, I find it most convenient to use Balaam's description, *Ahm* (people), since it not only conforms to historical usage but satisfies the need for a single word that can most aptly include the faith and folk elements. At the same time, this guide subscribes to *civilization* as the word that most definitively describes the totality of all that faith and folk have created.

2
WHAT WE DO—
AND DO NOT—
BELIEVE

i

Most religions turn to some writing, event, or personality for validation of beliefs and doctrines. The authoritative source to which we Jews turn for the original statement of our religious beliefs is what non-Jews refer to as the "Old Testament" (in contradistinction to the "New Testament"), and which is known to us as the *Tanakh* or Scriptures. The word *Tanakh* is an acronym for T*orah* (Pentateuch), N*eviim* (prophetic literature), and K*etuvim* (writings, i.e., remaining biblical books such as Psalms, Proverbs, etc.). The expression "Old Testament" is not employed because of theological considerations that, while of great importance to Christianity, are not acceptable to Jewish thought. Were "old" and "new" to be solely a matter of chronological appearance, there would be little of concern. But for the Christian, new and old carry with them implications of covenant between God and people. The new, for the Christian, is the fulfillment of the old. The new supersedes the old. The Jew cannot accept all that flows from this distinction.

However, it is not the entire Tanakh to which we turn for the validation of our doctrines but to the first five books, known in general usage as the Pentateuch, but known to Jewish tradition simply as the Torah, or teaching. Scattered throughout these first five books of the Bible are commandments, guidelines, and directives for man's use in his dealings with his fellowman, all of them validated as statements of God's will and disclosed through God's revelation to his spokesmen, foremost among whom was Moses.

But long before the laws and guidelines were formulated, the essential concepts of biblical thought with respect to the nature of God and man, and the relationships between them, were stated directly or by implication, within the framework of the first eleven chapters of the Book of Genesis. What emerges from those chapters is the fabric of belief about God and man, the relationship of God to man, and man's obligation to both God and his fellowman.

What of God? With the utmost simplicity, it is stated that "in the beginning, God created the heavens and the earth." God is the uncreated Creator. Independent of any prior forces out of whose substance he is caused to emerge, he is simply there, and by his will the universe takes on form as the act of creation unfolds step by step. There is nothing that owes its existence or its characteristics to any other cause save God's creative will.

Among the products of God's creative will is man. Two sentences in the story of man's creation are critical to our understanding of man: one in which it is stated that man was created in God's image (Gen. 1:27), and the other in which it is stated that God breathed into man "the breath of life" (Gen. 2:7). Through his receiving God's breath, it was man alone who was endowed with characteristics that put him into a special relationship to God.

But having thus posited the existence of an uncreated Creator-God who, as part of his creative act brings man into being and infuses him with something of himself, there must still be sought those characteristics of God that are descriptive of his nature. Until those characteristics are established, God is simply a Creator-God who could very well have had little interest in his handiwork aside from looking upon it with satisfaction.

At the outset of this inquiry, it is interesting to read in Genesis 2:9 that God placed in the Garden of Eden, along with "every tree that was pleasing to the sight and good for food," two other trees that were to play a critical role in the drama of man: "the tree of life in the middle of the garden, and the tree of knowledge of good and evil." By verse 17 the two trees have been combined into one, as far as their effect is concerned, for the eating of the fruit of the tree of knowledge of good and evil brings in its train the mortality of man: "for as soon as you eat of it, you shall be doomed to die."

The passage has important consequences for ultimate radical differences of theological doctrine. But the passage—indeed the story itself—also introduces the idea of the complete and absolute "otherness" of God. Eating of the tree of knowledge of good and evil can bring with it the additional danger reported in chapter 2, verse 22: "And the Lord God said, 'Now that man has become like one of us, knowing good and evil, what if he should stretch out his hand and take also from the tree of life, and live forever!' " In other words, while there is interaction between God and man, their respective realms must be recognized as forever appropriate to each. God acts in the world of man, but man is eternally man and must not presume to encroach upon God's powers. This is also the meaning of the Tower of Babel story, with which the first eleven chapters of Genesis come to an end. But the call for obedience to God's determination that man was not to reach for Godlike powers attributes to God no moral qualities.

It is in the story of Cain and Abel, and again in the story of Noah and the Flood, that the Jewish understanding of God's nature comes into view. In both instances, God takes punitive action because man has perpetrated acts of violence against his fellowman. He comes into full dimension as a God who is concerned about man's relationship to his fellowmen. It is in the earlier story, that of Cain and Abel (Gen. 4:7), that the implications of God's having breathed his spirit into man are spelled out: ". . . but if you do not do right, sin is the demon at the door [or, "crouches at the door"] whose urge is toward you; yet you can be his master."

The story, then, tells us not only of God's concern for man's moral behavior, but it also gives us the Jewish view of man's nature: On the one hand, there is the capacity for good—the good inclination—and on the other, the capacity for evil—the evil inclination. That which God has breathed into him did more than give him life; it gave him the power to cope with life. He is free to do either good or evil: ". . . sin crouches at the door, yet you can be its master." At a much later time, it will be written, "Everything is in the power of heaven except the fear of heaven." That is, man is given body, soul, mind. But he alone determines how he will use them. This view of man as an inherently free agent will have a direct bearing upon Judaism's inability to accept certain basic Christian doctrines.

Thus we see God as all-powerful and creative, the source of moral imperatives. When we give somewhat closer attention to the story of the Flood, we find additional elements of belief that have characterized Jewish thought. At the outset, man's wickedness (Gen. 6:5) caused God so to regret his creation of man, that he decided to destroy man and beast alike (Gen. 6:13). But, through Noah and his family, not only is man allowed to regenerate, but "the Lord said to himself: 'Never again will I doom the world because of man, since the devisings of man's mind are evil from his youth . . ." (Gen. 8:21). In just a few words, it is stated that God's mercy leads him to reconciliation with man, and a remnant, as it were, is permitted to survive punitive destruction, in order to regenerate mankind.

That man's thoughts are evil "from his youth" implies that the evil in man is not an active force until a particular stage in his personal growth. Indeed, in the traditional Jewish morning prayers, it is written, "My God, the soul you gave me came pure from You. . . ."

Thus, ranging over various stories from the Book of Genesis, we see in summation that God is one alone in the universe, moved by considerations of both justice and mercy, creating in man the totality of his humanness, and at the same time providing him with the spiritual means to cope with the destructive forces within himself. Man, therefore, is, by his very nature, in continuing spiritual tension, with neither inclination assuming dominance save to the extent that he will it so.

These first eleven chapters of Genesis are not Jewish history. They are the story of God and man, their respective roles in the universe, and their confrontations with each other. All of it is the foundation of our faith. All that follows the first eleven chapters of Genesis is footnote, commentary, and embodiment in the text of the Bible, of the moral and ethical teachings that flow from the Creation stories. Whether it be the Ten Commandments or the admonitions that immediately follow them; whether it be

Nathan's pointing the finger of accusation at David (2 Sam. 12:7) or Amos calling down God's doom upon the exploiters at Bethel, pleading for justice and righteousness (chapters 3 and 4); whether it be the psalmist evoking God's tender love (Ps. 103), or Micah projecting his vision of a world free of war (Mic. 4:1–4)—all trace their spiritual roots to Genesis.

All this, then, is at the heartland of what we Jews believe.

ii

In putting the question as to what we do not believe, I had in mind the need to answer the recurrent query: Why do Jews not believe in Jesus Christ? It is particularly appropriate to enter into discussion at this point, since the reply is intimately bound up with Jewish thought with respect to the nature of God and man.

In order to give proper reply to the question, it would make the response more understandable if the question were rephrased to read "Why do Jews not believe in Jesus as the Christ?" or perhaps "Why do Jews not accept Jesus as the Christ?" The question is rephrased in order to separate Jesus from his role as Christ, and thus better to present the Jewish position.

Thoughtful and knowledgeable Jews who are acquainted with the contents of the New Testament draw a distinction between the teachings *by* Jesus and the teachings *about* Jesus. In truth, there is nothing in Jesus' teachings or preachings that is at odds with Jewish ethical literature: They reflect an ethical impulse and quality of compassion to which it would be difficult to take exception—all the more so since the spirit of his teaching is imbued with the Jewish tradition within whose environment Jesus grew up. After all, it must not be lost sight of that Jesus, boy and man, was a Jew, exposed to the full range of the Jewish thought of his day. He was a habitué of the synagogues where he, like any other Jew was in touch with biblical books and their interpretations.

When asked (Mark 12:28) which commandment is first of all, Jesus replied with the words of Deuteronomy 6:4–5: "Hear O Israel! The Lord is our God . . . the Lord alone [or One Lord], and you are to love the Lord your God with all your heart, with all your soul and with all your strength." To which words he added these from Leviticus 19:18: "You shall love your neighbor as yourself."

Nothing could be more central to Jewish teaching and belief than these two quotations. And there are many other such evidences of Jesus' direct use or general reflection of biblical and postbiblical writings. Thus, his reply to the tempter in the desert (Matt. 4:3), "Man cannot live on bread alone; he lives on every word that God utters," is a verbatim quotation from Deuteronomy 8:3. In like manner, the Sermon on the Mount (Matt. 5) is replete with thoughts that find their parallel in biblical and postbiblical literature.

True, he was impatient with rabbinic law relating to certain aspects of Sabbath observance, and he challenged pharisaic concepts of purity, but it is certain that Jesus' objections were not to pharisaic doctrines as such but rather to excesses of expression and interpretation. After all, in his Sermon on the Mount, Jesus clearly states his commitment to the law and the prophets (Matt. 5:17–18).

True, his practice of proclaiming, "But verily *I* say to you . . . ," which is exemplified in the Sermon on the Mount, seems to indicate a sense of personal authority without regard to the rabbinic practice of placing authority within the framework of historical continuity (i.e. teacher to disciple) as formulated: "reporting a thing in the name of him who said it." But these did not become critical issues. At the most, those who looked to Jesus for whatever teaching and preaching he had to impart might conceivably have become a sect within the larger body of the Jewish religious community, but surely no more than that. In that event, Jesus would have lived and died as the leader of a splinter religious group.

But of course, to Christians, Jesus is far more than that. He is Jesus Christ. That is, he is Jesus the Christ. The designation Christ is the Greek equivalent of the Hebrew word *mashiah*, which means "anointed." Jesus the Christ is, therefore, "Jesus the Anointed."

In ancient Israel, kings, by the act of anointment, were validated in their selection. In 1 Samuel 15:1, Samuel said to Saul: "The Lord sent me to anoint you king over his people Israel." In 2 Samuel 5:3-4, it was "all the elders of Israel [who] came to the king at Hebron . . . and they anointed David king of Israel." Later, the Prophet Nathan is directed by God to inform David of the very special role he is to play in the history of Israel: "I took you from the pastures, and from following the sheep, to be prince over my people Israel. . . . I will make you a great name among the great ones of the earth. . . . The Lord has told you that he would build up your royal house. . . . Your family shall be established and your kingdom shall stand for all time in my sight, and your throne shall be established forever" (2 Sam. 7:8-16).

In the Jewish tradition of a restored and unified national sovereignty, it was always a descendant of David, prime symbol of the glorious days of old, who was destined to rule over the restored kingdom. And of course he would be *mashiah*, anointed, as a sign of his consecrated selection. But all this is national in character; there is no redemptive theological cast to it. Its concern is with the creation of an autonomous Jewish people, under a strong and beneficent ruler, dedicated to a just society within the larger framework of a secure and peaceful world wherein faith and folk can fulfill their interfabricated destiny. This Messiah/king of Davidic stock is well described in Isaiah 7:1-9.

However, Jesus as the Christ takes on a character that is completely alien to Jewish thought. It is that to which I referred earlier as "teachings about Jesus." For the drama of his life, his death on the cross, and his resurrection have a distinctly theological meaning, which, together with his identity as "God's only begotten Son" through whom "the world might be saved" (John 2:16-17) runs completely counter to Jewish understanding of the nature of God and of man, and of God's manifestation or self-revelation in the world of man.

It is exactly here that we are at the most critical parting of the ways. Throughout the entire body of our Scriptures, there is no evidence that God ever manifested himself in physical form. From the burning bush (Exod. 3:2) to the still, soft murmur (1 Kings 19:12), from the majestic array of the celestial bodies (Job 38) to the voice of revelation and prophetic mission uttered innumerable times, he was the unseen but ever-present God. He spoke *through* man, but never did he take on man's form. He enacts his will through man and through history, and that is the extent of it. For God to have placed himself in the world of man in the form of a Son was, in ancient times, as it is now, totally unacceptable to Jewish thought.

But this is only part of the problem. There remains what I have referred to as "the drama of the Cross." According to Christian doctrine, Jesus, as the Christ, had a foreordained mission; he had a role to play, for which he had been sent into the world. Through his sacrificial death, salvation became available to all who accepted him as redemptive Messiah. Paul preaches the doctrine of Christ as Savior in Romans 5 and 6. Through Christ, the sinner is saved from his condition of sin. "We know that the man we once were has been crucified with Christ, for the destruction of the sinful self, so that we may no longer be the slaves of sin, since a dead man is no longer answerable for his sins. But if we thus died with Christ, we believe that we shall also come to life with him" (Rom. 6:6–8).

There is some question as to whether Paul is saying that the condition of sin was the *inherited* effect of Adam's sin in the Garden of Eden; whether, that is, all humanity, for all time, inherited the taint of that original sin. He may simply be saying that Adam did indeed sin, but that it was only human mortality that became the heritage of all humanity.

But there is no question that by the time of Augustine (fourth century C.E.), the Christian concept of original sin as it is understood today received its essential formulation: "In Adam's fall, we sinnéd all."

For the Jew, this complex of beliefs, which give validation to the theological meaning of the Crucifixion, is precisely the point at which he parts company with Christianity. Quite apart from the initial nonacceptance of the idea that God could become incarnate and manifest himself in human form, the further system of thought built upon man's inherent taint finds no place in the Jewish view of the nature of man.

Men sin, but man does not come into the world a sinner standing in need of salvation. In an early homiletical commentary it is asked, "Why does a child of five, six, seven, eight, or nine years not sin, but only at ten years and upward? He himself gives strength to his evil inclination. *You* make your *yetzer* [evil inclination] bad." In our prayerbook, among the morning prayers it is written, "My God, the soul You gave me is pure." Sin comes when the individual, fully aware of the consequences of his acts, makes his decision in favor of the wrong. Two forces are forever in tension within man: the evil impulse and the impulse for good. Per se, the newborn infant or indeed the small child cannot be charged with the taint of sin. As the child matures and learns through teaching, example, and experience, he is better able to call into play that inner power with which God has endowed man and which is still the spiritual heritage of all men. Thus endowed, every human being is empowered to cope with the moral problems with which life confronts him.

Since there is none of us who does not fall short of the mark, through deliberate or unconscious wrongdoing, ways to atonement must be open. And for us as Jews, so they are, according to our interpretation of the nature of the human condition. But for the Jew, that way does not include the doctrine of a redeeming Savior. In the Jew's spiritual life, there is no place for a redemptive Christ, since his sacrificial death has no relevance for us within the framework of our beliefs about the nature of God and man.

Although *Yom Kippur* (Day of Atonement) has been set aside as *the* day of our religious calendar for the seeking of reconciliation with God, a rabbinic admonition counsels man to repent "one day before your death." The message is clear: Repentance should never await a ritual moment. As to the nature of repentance, the Jew is called upon to "turn back" from his sinful ways and, through repentance, charity, and prayer, to avert the stern decree of God. Atonement, therefore, is brought about through man's own efforts as he brings to bear that quality of soul with which God has endowed him. There is no intermediary between the Jew and his God. The drama of personal redemption must be acted out on the stage of this life where the sin has been perpetrated. The "charity" referred to above is to be understood in its original meaning of *caritas* (caring) which, for the Jew, must be translated into practical deeds of kindness (*g'milut hasadim*). The Jewish religious guidelines are replete with opportunities for such good deeds, which, in their performance, are the essence of the act of atonement.

Finally, closely related to the question of man's sinfulness are those related to retribution, to reward and punishment, as well as to heaven and hell. These latter questions are bound up with the question of immortality of the soul and of bodily resurrection. All of these problems have occupied man's thought for a very long time indeed. Quite apart from a natural curiosity about the nature of the hereafter, there was always the impelling need to be assured that life's inequities would somehow be rectified—if not in this world, then in the life to come.

It was of course inevitable that during the course of our history, from biblical times onward, Jewish thinkers should have reflected on these "ultimate" questions, as part of our concern about the meaning of man in the universe. But whatever positions were taken by our philosopher-theologians, it must be realized that in the absence of an official creed, we Jews have never been bound to the acceptance of doctrines on pain of forfeiting our identity as Jews or even as "religious" Jews.

To clarify: In the late twelfth century the great Jewish philosopher, Maimonides, formulated his Thirteen Articles of Faith, and these did include a statement of belief that God rewards those who fulfill the commandments of the Torah and punishes those who transgress them; there is also an affirmation of the resurrection of the dead. But although the Articles of Faith were a summation of views held over the centuries prior to Maimonides' lifetime, and his summation represented a consensus of the theological beliefs of his own generation, they never had, nor could have, "official" status, such as might be bestowed upon Christian doctrine by a church council, for there was no such official body in Jewish life. The authority of Jewish belief is rooted in the conviction—for those who hold it— that such teaching was part of the revelation at Sinai.

Belief in immortality of the soul found its way into the prayerbook, in phrases and blessings such as "Blessed art Thou O Lord who gives life to the dead," "and at the appointed time, Thou will take it [the soul] from this earth that it may enter upon life everlasting," and in the funeral ritual ("And may his [her] soul be bound up in the bond of life everlasting"). In addition, there are practices, such as the separate burial of severed or surgically removed organs, that relate to belief in the physical resurrection of the body. This practice is mandatory for any Jew who believes in such resurrection, but it is probable that most contemporary Jews do not hold to the doctrine of bodily resurrection. The new Reform prayerbook, as a matter of fact, has tended to play down even the concept of immortality of the soul and employs circumlocutions such as "return to the Reservoir of Being" and "Something of us can never die; we move in the eternal cycle of darkness and death, of light and life."

During the course of a television interview in 1973, the late Dr. Abraham Joshua Heschel, an eminent scholar and deeply spiritual man, said, "I think that's God's business what to do with me after life. Here, it's my business what to do with my life. So I leave it to him. I am so busy trying to lead a good life—and don't always succeed—that I have no time to worry about what God's going to do with me once I'm in the grave. Who knows what he expects of me in the grave?"

Heschel's statement reflects the "here and now" orientation of Jewish religious thought. If one lives as best one can, the future life will take care of itself. Notions about heaven are vague; a fiery hell is heavily discounted. For the most part, the way we Jews thought—and think—depended upon the influence of the cultures in which we found ourselves. Lacking an authoritative creed, a consensus might develop, and philosophers might attempt definitively to state normative fundamentals of Judaism. But in the end, there was little agreement upon such questions on the part of the average Jew. His chief concern, like Dr. Heschel's, was, and is, to live his life in accordance with God's will. What comes after will take care of itself.

3

VARIATIONS ON
A THEME

We have moved back and forth between Bible times and our own. We have spoken of religious thought rooted in the Torah, but reference has also been made to Jewish tradition and to the Rabbis who enunciated it. This section hopes to separate out those forces and factors that proved to be most formative as the Jew moved from Bible times into his postbiblical future.

i

The most incisively telling moment in the history of the Jewish people was undoubtedly at Sinai, when God entered into covenant with the Children of Israel. It was the first watershed in the historic development of the Jewish faith.

The second great watershed came about many hundreds of years later. If we place the Exodus at about the thirteenth century B.C.E. (before the common era), the second historic moment occurred during the sixth century B.C.E. Without a clear understanding of what occurred at that time, it is virtually impossible to understand the contemporary Jew. For with that event there came the beginning of transition from Judaism as biblical man practiced it to the Judaism of postbiblical times, even though "biblical times" had not as yet run their course.

The critical event that brought about such a radical change was the Babylonian exile, an event that the prophets of that period had interpreted as an impending, and then a fulfilled, punishment visited upon the people for their failure to carry out the terms of their covenant/treaty with the Lord. Israel had already been severely reduced in 721 B.C.E. when the Assyrians sent into exile virtually the entire northern kingdom. With the Babylonian exile, the southern kingdom of Judah ceased to exist; the Temple was destroyed and Jerusalem was made defenseless.

The effect was traumatic. The people were separated from land and sanctuary, a state of affairs they could scarcely believe God would have perpetrated on his people, his land, his sanctuary. But despite their shocked disbelief, they maintained a stubborn resistance to abandoning the now deeply rooted historic monotheism. Encouraged by the hopeful messages of the prophets of the exile—especially the Isaiah of chapters 40–66—and utilizing new forms of worship as a substitute for the lost Temple and sacrificial practices, they realized in their despair that the messages of the prophets had rung true. As the exile drew to an end after fifty years (538 B.C.E.), due to the triumph of the Persians over the Babylonians, coupled with the favorable disposition of Cyrus toward the Jews (Ezra 1:1–4), preparation had been made for the regeneration of the old covenantal relationship with God. But it was to be a regeneration with a profoundly marked difference.

There was now no doubt that God was determined not

to tolerate faithlessness in any form. At the same time, the prophetic insistence that the moral component in worship of, or homage to, God, while not a replacement for worship, was still superior to it left in its wake a great question in the minds of the chastened people: How do we begin again? What are we to do?

The beginning of the answer to that question was undertaken by Ezra, a late migrant back to the Holy Land. Described as of priestly descent, a scribe, and "learned in the law of Moses" (Ezra 7:1–6), he had "devoted himself to the study and observance of the Law of the Lord, and to teaching statute and ordinance in Israel" (Ezra 7:10). This very important statement clearly suggests that even before Ezra returned to the land, the books of the Pentateuch either had been, or were being, assembled into final form as we know them today, and that the role of the scribe was that of interpreter and teacher.

The story of events recorded in the eighth through tenth chapters of Nehemiah carries the process of covenantal regeneration to its conclusion. The "book of the law of God" is read to the people in the presence of Nehemiah and the other notables who flank Ezra as he reads. That the effect was dramatic is an understatement. At the conclusion of the lengthy reading, and the interpretation of its meaning in terms of a detailed review of Israel's history to that date, a new covenant was signed and sealed. The wording is of critical importance: "The rest of the people . . . who are capable of understanding, and all who for the sake of God have kept themselves apart from the foreign population, join with the leading brethren when the oath is put to them, swearing to obey God's law given by Moses, the servant of God, and to observe and to fulfill all the commandments of the Lord our God, His rules and His statutes" (Neh. 10:28, 29).

Almost eight hundred years had passed since the first covenant at Sinai—and now a new covenant. But there is a difference. At Sinai, the Book of the Torah was not yet formulated. Now, with Ezra, we have begun anew. As we noted in the words that introduced this guide, Balaam described Israel as a people who dwell alone, who do not reckon themselves among the nations. The words of the second covenant underscore Balaam's description. Israel has indeed consciously undertaken an act of separation— not as an act of elitist snobbery but as a determined move to preserve the purity of the old monotheism and with singlemindedness "to observe and fulfill all the command- ments of the Lord our God, His rules and His statutes."

ii

What does all this mean for our story of the Jewish faith and folk? It means that with Ezra we witness the beginning of the end of both priest and prophet as primary spokes- men for Israel's relationship to God. In place of both, there is the beginning of a tradition that has reached into our own day: the preeminent authority of the teacher and in- terpreter of the Book. With the supplanting of the prophet by the teacher-preacher, we are introduced to the seedling Judaism, whose growth will radically affect the practices, beliefs, and institutions of Jewish life for the next two mil- lennia. The last prophetic voices were heard during the Babylonian exile, and only briefly thereafter. They are words of hope and confidence, of rejoicing over the resto- ration of Jerusalem. The voice of Malachi, the last of the literary prophets, and probably a contemporary of Ezra, conveys the spirit of the times. He questions the right of the priests to act as interpreters of God's word, hammers against the still prevailing practice of "marrying daughters of a foreign God," and exhorts the people toward a more compassionate family morality. But already the prophet seems to be in part a teacher, for his statements are in reply to questions encountered: "You ask why. . . ." "You ask, 'How have we wearied him . . . ?' " "You ask, 'How have we defrauded you [God] . . . ?' " "You ask, 'How can we return . . . ?' " This has the quality of a dialogic exchange (Mal. 2:17; 3:8, 13, 14).

Here is the mood of practical righteousness, the old spirit of Amos when he inveighed against exploitation. The old prophets were the architects of the grand edifice of Israel's proper relationship to God; theirs was the blueprint of a people and a world order under the aegis of God. The priests' way provided reconciliation through sacrifice; the prophets' way, reconciliation through righteousness. History had now provided the momentum for the building of an edifice that, stone by stone and brick by brick, would give body to the old blueprints, by applying to the workaday life of the individual Jew guidelines for carrying out God's purposes as revealed through the Book, the Torah. The new password was: "To be what you must be as Jews, this is what you must do as Jews."

R. Travers Hereford, in his *Pharisaism*, states it well: "And therefore, when Ezra prevailed on the Jews to become a separate community, he was not condemning them to a life of barren legalism, cutting them off from a free communion with God; he was providing for them a means whereby they could enjoy that free communion, defended against the dangers which in the past had been so disastrous to the religious life of the people. . . . It is indeed difficult to believe that they would have survived, if the policy of Ezra had not been carried out."

What was that policy? To make of the people the people

of the Book; to make the study of God's law central to their lives, their understanding of the way to God; to provide a method whereby no aspects of the individual's life could or would remain untouched by God's will as revealed through the Torah—and *torah*, it must be understood, simply means "teaching." Out of its exploration could and did emerge many norms for man's guidance, some of them with the force of law. The new covenant called for total reconstruction of the person and the people.

iii

The method of Ezra the Scribe, which began during the exile and continued after his return, was carried on for hundreds of years. Out of the generations-long effort was created a sizable body of interpretations, sermonic parables, laws—the kind of guidance a people would and did rely on for personal and collective regulation of life in all its manifold aspects.

The tradition begun by Ezra, then, led to the ultimate creation of a large collection of teachings, both legal and theological, whose formulation was principally the product of Rabbis (*rabbi* = my master = teacher/scholar) and rabbinic academies, from the first century B.C.E. to the fifth century C.E.

The rabbinic teaching and legal formulations were based upon a revolutionary new concept of the nature of God's revelation—a concept to which all our contemporary Jewish religious thought and practice is indebted. That concept was the doctrine of the "Oral Torah," which held that simultaneously with the giving of the Torah to Moses at Sinai there was also given a separate body of law and guidelines which, though oral rather than written, was of equal sanctity and validity. The doctrine was a creation of the Pharisees, and its net effect, in the words of a Christian scholar, Rosemary Radford Reuther, was "to free Israel from the letter of the past and to find an opening into new futures, while simultaneously making it their intention to preserve every jot and tittle of that past itself. The Oral Torah was intended to remain oral, to be embodied in the living stream of a people, not in document, even though it eventually was given written form."

Thus there entered into the mainstream of Jewish thought some ideas and doctrines that are not to be found in the written Torah: Life after death, reward and punishment, fixed and mandatory prayer, the personalization of God's salvation through meritorious acts. The Pharisees and then their "continuators" (Jacob Neusner's designation), the Rabbis, pointed the way for the observant Jew to become the spiritual Jew. With the destruction of the second Temple in 70 C.E., the Rabbis developed teachings that in effect made every man a potential priest and every table an altar.

Their labors bore good fruit. By creating and preserving new guidelines in the form of religious law and spiritual perception, they made it possible for the Jewish folk and faith to survive and then to surmount the fall of the Temple.

By the second century C.E. the voluminous bulk of rabbinic teaching was in need of structured organization into its component categories, and thus it came about that there was put together into appropriate tractates a compendium known as the *Mishnah* (teaching). Additional centuries of discussion and analysis based upon the Mishnah brought into being a further compendium known as the *Gemara* (study, i.e., of the Mishnah). In the sixth century C.E. Mishnah and Gemara were combined to make up that definitive body of literature we know as the *Talmud*.

iv

What is the Talmud, and what does it mean as an aid to the understanding of Jewish faith and folk?

As brief and as simplified as our account of the growth of postbiblical Judaism has been, it is hoped that the following development has been evident: Mediated by generations of teachers and scholars, beginning with Ezra, the Torah—the Book—assumed a preeminence it has never lost. Judaism became the religion of the Book. But Torah was now to be understood not only in terms of its own written text, the five books of the Pentateuch, but even more largely in terms of that ultimately massive compilation based upon the doctrine of the Oral Law, which found its ultimate statement in the Talmud. Torah was now not merely a book—it was a literature inclusive of all the legal and homiletical/theological writings that had grown out of it. It was well stated in one of the tractates of the Talmud: "Turn it over [i.e., the Torah] and turn it over again, for everything is in it."

The process that began with Ezra and ended with the completion of the Talmud took about a thousand years. But that millennium created for our people a guide for both personal and collective life, which provided a firm foundation for religious practice, personal morality, and community institutions. Over that millennium, guidance was created, relating to Sabbath, festival and holy days observance, personal purity, cohesive home life, social justice, business practices, the cycle of life from birth to death, and all other aspects of the civilization the Jewish people had become.

It established for our dispersed people a "portable homeland" to such an extent that every Jewish community, no matter where established, had in the Talmud and its commentaries a remarkable instrument through which virtually all of its felt needs could be met. No matter where a Jew might travel, he would find in every Jewish community just that—a community, a structure that was closely comparable to every other community. He was home.

As noted earlier, the rabbinic tradition assured the survival of the Jewish faith and folk, by creating a highly imaginative and effective approach to religious and folk expression in the midst of alien environments. Balaam's description had come true in a way surely beyond his wildest capacity to envision.

Although the Talmud has long since been completed, the principle of rabbinic tradition has continued. New problems, during the past thousand years but more largely during the past few centuries, have been brought to the attention of recognized rabbinic scholars who, probing Torah, Talmud, and then, as time went on, studying each other's findings, have offered answers. These questions and their replies are to be found in a body of Jewish literature known as *Responsa*. While you read this guide, it is safe to say that throughout the Jewish world such questions and answers are going back and forth between inquirers and rabbinic authorities. For those Jews who wish to live in full accord with Jewish tradition and law, it is of vital importance to know what positions have been taken with respect to such varied problems as artificial insemination, photoelectric cells as automatic Sabbath light kindlers, autopsy, birth control and abortion, certain additives in food, enforced work on Sabbath and/or holy days, and an abundance of others. As from the beginning, the concern is to adapt where possible to changing times, while holding as firmly as possible to original principles.

From its inception, the process has not been unlike that of the Supreme Court of the United States in its interpretations of the intention and meaning of our Constitution. Out of their deliberations, there has arisen a voluminous body of law whose intent has been to respond to current problems, in terms of a document whose framers surely could never have imagined the various forces and factors of our complex civilization, as we are now experiencing them.

v

Rabbinic Judaism, or as we might now call it, traditional Judaism, was firmly seated until modern times. It was the only expression of our religious beliefs and practices.

Following the French revolution, with its slogan of "Liberty, Equality, Fraternity," restrictions against Jews in areas affected by the revolution slowly came to an end. A world of larger opportunity opened to us, so that access to the thought and culture of Western Europe was increasingly wide open. As a result, secular studies at the universities, coupled with a compelling desire to integrate into the cultural life of society, brought about radical changes in Jewish thought and religious expression. It was the Age of Enlightenment, the Age of Reason, and there were numerous leaders in Jewish life, especially in Germany, who felt that traditional forms and practices that could not meet the needs of modern thought, as exemplified by the word *reason*, must be reassessed and reformulated.

As a result, first laymen and then rabbinic leaders undertook to effect reforms in the conduct of religious worship and ritual practices. The traditional *siddur* (book of prayer) was abbreviated and translated into the language of the land; instrumental music—prohibited since the destruction of the Temple in Jerusalem as a sign of mourning—was introduced; family seating was made a standard practice (traditionally, women had occupied a separate section of the sanctuary); the validity of bar mitzvah and even of circumcision, the wearing of the *talit* (prayer shawl), as well as covering of the head during worship—all these were subjected to vigorous debate.

Out of this reexamination of the binding nature of rabbinic tradition, came the founding and development of what we know today as Reform Judaism, whose basic doctrine respecting traditional Judaism was that rabbinic authority as expressed in talmudic practice and doctrine was no longer valid. It was therefore held possible, desirable, and necessary to bring Judaism into the new day if it was to meet the demands of reason and enlightenment and of the new generation, which, heady with the new liberation, looked upon the old forms of religious expression as outlandish when compared with the prevailing practices of their Christian friends.

Whatever the more superficial aspects of assimilation, at the heart of the religious philosophy of the reformulation was the denial of the origin of the Oral Law—implicit meaning in the Written Law—and therefore denial of the entire body of rabbinic teaching as validated by God at Sinai. Save for this observation, the whole experience bears comparison with the great reformulations of Catholic practice in both popular and papal statement, during the third quarter of the twentieth century, known as the process of *aggiornamento*—literally, "updating." The translation of the mass into English or other vernaculars, the raising of the issue of priestly celibacy versus marriage, alternative practices in worship forms, the quiet rebellion against the ban on abortion, nonrhythm birth control, the setting aside by some orders of nuns of their traditional habits in favor of modern dress, the participation of religious orders in social action programs (vigils, marches, picketing, etc.)—all give us a sense of the ferment that brought Reform Judaism into being in its own time, the 1830s.

The third great stream of Jewish religious change found expression in what we know today as Conservative Judaism, which, in its beginnings, called itself Historical Judaism. Conservative Judaism, while in many ways closely related to Reform Judaism, has held that there is need for a liberal Judaism closer to the spirit, intention, and practice of traditional Judaism—to which the designation "Orthodox" is now generally given. Conservative Judaism accepted the principle of family seating, translation of the prayerbook into English, as well as, here and there, the introduction of instrumental music into the synagogue. On the other hand, it adhered in principle and practice to the tradition of the covering of the head during worship, the retention of bar mitzvah, cantillation of prayers and biblical readings in worship, observance of *kashrut* (dietary laws), the greater use of Hebrew in the services, Sabbath laws, and similar traditional practices.

This is not to state that Reform and Conservative Judaism are as divergent today as they were at the founding of American Conservative Judaism in the late nineteenth century. To the contrary, there are clear evidences of Reform's increasing return to traditional practices, as well as of Conservatism's acceptance of such nontraditional practices as permitting women to take part in worship procedures on the dais, and to be counted in the quorum for congregational worship (*minyan*).

Without doubt it is in the very nature of our changing climate of opinion with respect to the nature and obligation of religious practice, coupled with deep-seated psychological needs answered through such practice, that time will see further adjustments in both Reform and Conservative Judaism. But today Conservatism's essential difference from Reform is that it holds *halakhah* (rabbinic law) to be binding to the extent that changes in religious practice, to be acceptable, must be halakhically based.

4

OF TIME, FEASTS, FESTIVALS, HOLY DAYS

i

As I write these words, it is the year 5737 according to the Jewish calendar, which means that according to ancient reckoning, it has been 5737 years since the creation of the world. This figure was arrived at by computing backward from known dates, through reported life-spans of biblical personalities and genealogical "begats." When designating the civil year, it has become customary for Jews to replace B.C. (before Christ) and A.D. (*Anno Domini*—in the year of the Lord) with B.C.E. (before the common era) and C.E. (the common era).

The Jewish calendar is based upon the phases of the moon as it encircles the earth, but it is also adjusted to the solar year. It is therefore referred to as "lunisolar."

Since the duration of a lunar month is 29½ days, there are 354 days in the lunar year. Obviously, the lunar year falls short of the solar year, based upon the movement of the earth around the sun, by eleven days. An adjustment has to be made periodically to bring the lunar year into harmony with the solar year. This is done by introducing an additional month at precalculated intervals, which is given the same name as the last month of the lunar year, but noted as "second." Since the closing month of the Jewish calendar is Adar, the leap month is referred to as *Adar Sheni*, second Adar.

The names of the months are Nisan, Iyar (Eeyar), Sivan, Tamuz, Ab, Elul, Tishri, Heshvan, Kislev, Tevet (Tay-vet), Sh'vat, Adar. The *h* in Heshvan has a somewhat gutteral sound akin to the small noise we make when trying to dislodge a very small fishbone from our throat. Nisan roughly coincides with April, although because of the lunar year, it can fall back to March.

The day is reckoned as beginning with sundown and extending to the next sundown. The week is made up of seven days, the first six of which are known simply by number—first day, second day, etc. The seventh day, Saturday, which begins at sundown on Friday, is known as *Shabbat*, Sabbath (rest).

It is the purpose of this section of the guide to describe the festivals and holy days of the Jewish year, but instead of listing them in terms of time sequence, they will be grouped in such a way that their character will be more clearly understood. The groupings yield us three categories: agricultural-historical, historical, and what can best be described as "spiritual." There is one festival that does not lend itself to any of these categories, *Simhat Torah*, but it is certainly related to all of them, since it celebrates the completion and renewal of the cycle of readings from the Torah. It will receive a fuller description when we come to its place in the calendar.

ii

The best vantage point from which to enter into the Jewish year is Exodus 23:14–17. "Three times a year you shall hold a festival for Me: You shall observe the Feast of Unleavened Bread—eating unleavened bread for seven days as I have commanded you—at the set time in the month of Abib, for in it you went forth from Egypt . . . and the Feast of the Harvest of the first fruits of your work, of what you sow in the field; and the Feast of Ingathering at the end of the year, when you gather in the results of your work from the field. Three times a year all your males shall appear before the Lord God."

The last verse of the foregoing quotation tells us why these three festivals were known as "pilgrimage festivals." They are known to us by name as *Pesah, Shavuot,* and *Sukkot.* Their English designations are: Passover, Festival of Weeks, and Harvest Festival, respectively. The latter is known as the Festival of Booths: It is not the intention of this guide to go into historical study of these festivals; suffice it to say that the biblical sources clearly state their agricultural roots. The Jewish historical association is most strongly stated in chapter 12 of Exodus, particularly verse 17: ". . . for on this very day I brought your ranks out of the land of Egypt; you shall observe this day throughout the generations as an institution for all time." It is in this chapter, also, that Passover's month was ordained to be "the beginning of the months; it shall be the first of the months of the year for you" (12:2).

That the three festivals are traditionally so strongly related to the Exodus underscores the intensity of meaning that historical event held for us. The old agricultural elements in the pilgrimage festivals still survive in our own time. What is most important is that whatever the original root of each festival, the Jewish religious genius translated their meaning to conform to our historic consciousness and emphasis. The Exodus stands as the primary event in our history, overriding all others.

iii

Passover, the first of the three pilgrimage festivals, beginning as it does on Nisan 15, is also the first festival of the Jewish calendar year.

How much of ancient practice still finds expression in our own time? Remarkably, quite a lot. While later historical necessity extended the original seven days to eight (Reform Jewry observes only seven), basic injunctions relating to Passover are still given considerable attention. The law requiring a lamb or kid to be sacrificed as a paschal offering has long since been inoperative, but the eating of *matzot* (unleavened bread) is still more or less faithfully observed. By "more or less" is meant that there are degrees of scrupulousness, depending on just where in the spectrum of religious or ritual observance the individual prefers to locate himself. This is true of all religious observance: Differences will distinguish the Reform or Liberal Jew from his more traditional fellow Jew.

For the purposes of this guide, Jewish ritual practice will be described in terms of the more traditional procedures.

Anyone who has had association with a Jewish household knows the air of excitement and anticipation that the coming of Passover engenders. Ingredients for traditional Passover foods must be purchased, and the house cleared of all leaven in sufficient time so that not even a crumb will contaminate the Passover purity. The guidelines for what food is permitted and what is forbidden in the home during Passover are quite specific and list a number of grains that are subject to fermentation. The definition of leaven goes beyond the activating ingredient of yeast or sourdough. For the observant Jew, the rules are faithfully observed. Where supervision of mechanical processes in the preparation of food and drink for Passover can be arranged, only that which has been duly validated by recognized rabbinic authority for such use is purchased for Passover utilization.

Not only does the house undergo the equivalent of a traditional spring housecleaning but, for the fully observant, dishes utilized only on Passover are brought out of storage. Pots and pans, the stove itself, will be thoroughly cleansed so that no vestige of *hametz* (*hahmetz* = leaven) remains. Thus is carried out the biblical injunction: "No leaven shall be found in your houses for seven days" (Exod. 12:19).

The principal event of the Passover week is the ritual supper, which occurs on the eves of the first two days for the traditional Jew and on the eve of the first day alone for most Reform Jews. While the first two and concluding two days of Passover are marked by special services in the synagogue, it is the home ceremony that is the high point of Passover observance. In a manner of speaking, the climax of the Passover season occurs at its outset. Many congregations hold community seders, and while any non-Jew is a welcome guest at each seder, there are families whose second seder is specifically designed to be an ecumenical experience. This is equally applicable to the community seder.

Since the seder is thought by most Christians to have been Jesus' last supper, many churches have adopted the custom of celebrating a Passover supper, and to that end have borrowed key elements from Jewish tradition.

The supper itself is called the *seder* (order); the reference is to the order of the service. The text for the table service is known as the *Haggadah* (account). In its text, the reason for celebrating the Passover is related, and the meaning of the Passover symbols explained—all graced with song and with questions and answers designed to keep the attention of the children during the somewhat protracted goings-on before and after the meal itself. As a matter of fact, the Haggadah as it has come down to us is very much a children's as well as an adult's primer of Jewish history. It has been customary to illustrate the text in such a way that even the youngest child can understand something of the story of Passover. The Haggadah was designed to fulfill the injunction that each Jew should relate to his child the events of the Exodus. The words of the text read: "In every generation, one ought to regard himself as though he had personally come out of Egypt. As it is said, 'And thou shalt tell thy son on that day, saying, "This is on account of what the Lord did for me when I went forth from Egypt." ' "

How the children look forward to this evening! A mood of both awe and excitement surrounds them. They patiently endure the parts of the service in which they do not themselves share, knowing that there will come the moment when the youngest who is capable of doing so will be called on to recite or chant the Four Questions (really, one question repeated four times, but with four different answers): "Why is this night different from all other nights? On all other nights we may eat both leavened and unleavened bread; tonight only unleavened bread. On all other nights we eat all kinds of herbs; tonight only bitter herbs. On all other nights we do not dip even once; tonight we dip twice. On all other nights, sit either straight or reclining; tonight we all recline."

There will be other such moments when they can join in

with vocal fervor, such as the "Dayenu" (Dahyaynu), meaning "it would have been sufficient," which is the antiphonal response to recitation of each of a succession of blessings God bestowed upon the Israelites: "Had He given us the Sabbath and not brought us near Him at Mount Sinai, it would have been sufficient! Had He brought us near Him and not given us the Torah, it would have been sufficient!"

And so on, throughout the seder, from the gay search for the hidden *aphikomen*, a piece of *matzah* hidden early in the service to be found and redeemed at a later moment, to the singing of that strangely fascinating "Had Gadya" (An Only Kid) and "Ehad Mi Yodayah" (Who Knows One?).

The table is set and ready. A ceremonial plate has been set at the leader's chair, itself complete with pillow on which he will lean—a privilege that ancient Roman custom conferred on the free man. Thus is denoted the meaning of Passover as a festival of freedom. On the plate there will be placed a roasted egg, a lamb's shank bone, bitter herbs (horseradish or ordinary radish), a green such as parsley, and *haroset*. This last is a mixture of chopped apples and nuts, with seasoning of cinnamon and wine. There will also be available a container of salt water, and a plate or special matzah cover containing three matzot.

Matzot, haroset, greens, bitter herbs, and an egg (hard-boiled) will be at the place of each participant. Finally, there will be at everyone's place a wine goblet, with an additional "Cup of Elijah" on the table.

As the seder proceeds, the tale of ancient days is told through both word and symbol. Even the required four cups of wine have their meaning. Thus, in Exodus 6:6–7, God's redemption of Israel is mentioned in four different ways: "I will free you . . . and deliver you. . . . I will

Leader's Passover plate, antique design

redeem you. . . . I will take you to be my People." It has been suggested that the promise in verse 8, "I will bring you into the Land," gave rise to the tradition of the fifth cup, the Cup of Elijah; Elijah has long been the hero of popular tales associated with the regeneration of the Jewish people, and the house door is opened for him during the course of the service.

The matzah—"bread of affliction"—bespeaks the haste in which the Hebrews left Egypt; the haroset symbolizes the mortar used by the Israelites when building the Egyptian cities. *Karpas* (greens) is an obvious sign of the earth's renewal, although the salt water in which it is dipped, representing as it does our tears, moderates and historicizes the ancient agricultural element. Just as the karpas is a symbol of springtime, so also is the egg, but, again, the nature element has been historicized by having the roasted egg symbolize the ancient Temple festival sacrifice known as the *Hagigah*. Finally, there remain the bitter herbs and the shank bone: The former are clearly symbolic of Israelite experience in Egypt; the latter replaces the paschal lamb.

The first part of the service completed, the festive meal is served, complete with foods so long associated with the seder: gefillte fish, matzah ball soup, and chicken. It is the housewife's special opportunity to show her culinary skills.

The service is resumed after grace, and one more joyous festival concludes. Many a Jew who in adult life has become less attentive to religious practices still recalls with fond memory the seder, when a very special aura enveloped father and mother, when special guests sat at table with more familiar friends and family, when the special appointments of linen and silverware shone with unaccustomed brightness, and festive candles gave forth an extra radiance.

Shavuot, the Feast of Weeks, is the second of the pilgrimage festivals, and although strongly agricultural in its origin has, typically, taken on a distinctively Jewish religiohistoric meaning. A number of biblical passages refer to this festival: Exodus 23:16, Leviticus 23:15, Deuteronomy 16:9–10, and Deuteronomy 26. Traces of Shavuot in Christian practice are to be seen in the celebration of Pentecost, fifty days after Easter. For the Jew, Shavuot commemorates and celebrates the principal event of the Exodus: the revelation of God's law at Mt. Sinai. In the symbolic statement of our faith, the Ten Commandments were the "first fruits" of our religious experience as a people. Known to us as the "season of the giving of the Torah," Shavuot even in biblical times combined both agricultural and folk-historical elements, but in a way that coupled nature, reminiscence, and the sense of covenant destiny. Deuteronomy 26 is fully descriptive of this interfabrication of the different strands of our self-awareness in those days.

The ceremony described in Deuteronomy 26 was one of affirmation by the individual of his indebtedness to God for his liberation, for the good land, "flowing with milk and honey," and his commitment to "walk in His ways . . . and to hearken to His voice."

This call to folk/God renewal finds its modern expression in the ceremony of confirmation.

It is traditional on Shavuot to eat dairy foods. There is no firmly proven reason why this is so, but it is thought that perhaps the practice grew out of the reference in Deuteronomy 26:15 to the "land flowing with milk and honey."

It is with *Sukkot*, the Festival of Tabernacles or Booths, that the three pilgrimage festivals conclude. Its biblical references are Leviticus 23:33–36, 39–43; Exodus 23:16, 24:32; and Deuteronomy 16:13–15.

What is especially interesting about Sukkot is that in addition to the biblical association of both agricultural and historical elements, there is what can best be called a tribute to the beauty of nature. That biblical man was attuned to nature in all its manifold aspects is attested to throughout the Psalms. As spare as is the biblical explanation of the connection between Sukkot and Jewish history, it still echoes with the intensity of joyful celebration that animated it ever since its biblical beginnings. It summons the Jew to a total celebration of God in the world. What is especially stirring to the reflective Jew is that though in its essential form Sukkot called upon him to commemorate the days of passage from Egypt to the Promised Land at the very season of the year when the riches of the harvest would most strongly contrast with the rigors of desert life, the land and the harvest alike were celebrated long after the people were dispersed from both land and harvest. It is no wonder that Sukkot is called "the season of our rejoicing." Memory of time past and hope for restoration have been intimately bound up together in the festival of Sukkot.

The principal features of the festival are twofold: the *sukkah* itself, and *lulav* and *etrog*.

As far as its construction is concerned, the sukkah may be either a sort of lean-to attached to a dwelling, or a separate structure. There are rabbinical laws relating to the construction of the sukkah, the principal one of which has to do with how the roof itself is made, since therein is to be found its essential frailty, open as it must be to the elements. In this way, the temporary nature of our dwellings en route to Canaan is symbolized. During the seven days of Sukkot, traditionalists following the biblical precept to "dwell in sukkot" make a practice of eating as many meals therein as possible. The building of a sukkah, its adornment with fruits and wall decorations, its hallowing through appropriate blessings, its utilization for meals—all are the measure of the commitment or noncommitment of the modern Jew to time-honored and rabbinically regulated traditions and laws.

The building of a sukkah is still widely practiced. Where it is placed will of course depend on what space is available for its construction. Portable sukkot, simple to assemble and take down, are available; congregations sometimes erect elaborate constructions on their grounds or sometimes within the sanctuary. It is not unusual for Jewish students to arrange for the building of a sukkah on their campuses. In many instances, the sukkah has become miniaturized into models that can be used as table centerpieces. In all instances, every effort is made to fashion a structure of beauty in keeping with the spirit of the festival.

The second principal feature of Sukkot is what is sometimes referred to as "the four species," and which I called lulav and etrog—the names by which they are traditionally known. Leviticus 23:40, the source for their use, refers to the citron tree, the palm, the myrtle, and the willow of the brook. The first is represented by the citron, a lemon-like fruit with delicate aroma; the palm is used in its enfolded state and bound together with the myrtle and willow. These three in combination are known as the lulav. The lulav is in actuality the designation of the palm branch alone, but since it is the largest of the three and dominates the unit, it gives its name to the entire ensemble.

Although in an older day every traditional Jew considered it desirable to acquire a lulav and etrog for himself, contemporary practice has neglected this custom. But it is very unlikely that any temple or synagogue is without them in order to celebrate Sukkot appropriately, for they are an integral part of the worship service. In the daily traditional liturgy, they are waved to the four points of the compass—an indication of God's omnipresence—at that point in the service where psalms of praise to God, known as the *Hallel*, are read.

With Sukkot, the cycle of pilgrimage festivals comes to an end. The occasions have served the Jew well by answering both the need to maintain harmonious relationship with the fruitful earth and the even deeper need to retell the nature of God's relationship to his people.

iv

Two other holidays of the Jewish calendar repeat the theme of folk salvation through God's manifestation at crucial moments in our history. The Exodus and its subsequent events had to do with the birth of a people, as it were, and its convenant with God. The two holidays referred to concern two threats of crisis proportion, which came to naught, against both faith and folk. In both instances, God's role is implied rather than articulated as such. The holidays I am referring to are known as *Hanukkah* and *Purim*.

Hanukkah falls on the twenty-fifth day of the month of Kislev and is observed for eight days. Kislev is a midwinter month, and because our lunar calendar moves about a bit in relationship to the solar calendar, Hanuk-kah occasionally coincides with Christmas. This, plus the additional fact that in its externals it is a festival of lights and gift-giving, has led to a common Christian belief that Hanukkah is "the Jewish Christmas'."

However, this interpretation is quite mistaken. As everyone knows, of course, Christmas celebrates the birth of Jesus. On the other hand, Hanukkah commemorates a historic event dating from the year 165 B.C.E., the con-tributing factors of which are recounted in the First Book of Maccabees, which can be found in the Apocrypha.

The event referred to was the rededication of the Tem-ple in Jerusalem following a dogged military struggle against the Greek-Syrian ruler of Palestine, Antiochus. His attempts to change the Jewish character of the land by introducing alien customs and by striking at the very roots of Jewish religious practices threatened the con-tinued existence of Judaism. Judah Maccabee became the charismatic leader under whose banner resistance led to ultimate victory. "Then Judas, his brothers, and the whole congregation of Israel decreed that the rededication of the altar should be observed with joy and gladness at the same season each year, for eight days, beginning on the twenty-fifth of Kislev" (1 Macc. 4:59).

Hanukkah is traditionally observed with the lighting of candles and, more recently, by exchange of gifts within the family. The candelabrum, know as a *menorah* (literal translation of candelabrum) or, in fuller expression, as a Hanukkah menorah in distinction to the Sabbath meno-rah, is also called a *Hanukkiah*, in contemporary usage. Unlike the Sabbath candelabrum, which holds seven can-dles, the Hanukkiah holds nine, one of which is known as the *shamash* (servitor), whose function is to kindle the other candles. In an older day, although not too far re-

Hanukkah Menorah

moved from our own time, the Hanukkah menorah was an oil lamp with nine small receptacles, and was often a beautiful example of the silversmith's art.

The practice is as follows: One candle is kindled the first night, two the second, and so on, with traditional blessings. The mood of Hanukkah is gay and festive, with the evening adorned with song amid the excitement of opening packages. In the religious school, the festival will be further marked with song, plays, and festal programs. All in all, it is an occasion of great spirit.

Hanukkah's traditional food is the potato *latke* which is simply a pancake made of grated potatoes. I'm not aware of any historical reasons for eating latkes on Hanukkah, but agree with all who find it a delightful adjunct to a festive holiday.

Here too, then, as with Purim, a description of which will follow, we celebrate God's manifestation in our folk fortunes. For us, history is not just "something that happened." It is not just the solitary spirit of the individual that is moved by God in the world, but nations as well. Thus many of our holy days and festivals celebrate God's intervention in the life of man.

The last of the holidays that celebrate that intervention is *Purim*. In the one day it is celebrated, the fourteenth of Adar, is contained a veritable outpouring of mirth and fun. Marked in the synagogue by the reading of the scroll of the Book of Esther, full opportuntiy is given for the expression of joyous excitement. In the synagogue itself, at the time of the reading, the young people present are afforded opportunity to make a bit of noise with their *greggers*—a kind of racheted spool against which a tongue rasps when the hand-held device is whirled about—whenever the name of the arch-villain Haman is mentioned in the narrative. (Those familiar with the biblical story in the Book of Esther will recall that Haman plotted the destruction of the Jews. The noise of the greggers was to drown out the very sound of his name.) Lacking a gregger, any noisemaker will do. Needless to say, it takes quite a bit of doing to keep a balance between desired sanctuary decorum and the young people's need for release.

There is a long tradition of carnival for Purim. Spirits are high, and in an older day, "Purim spielers," troupes of merrymakers who enacted events from the story of Purim, were common. Today most, if not all, of this tradition is preserved in the religious school or Hebrew school, in the form of dramatics, skits, folk dancing, masquerade, and the like.

At the conclusion of the story in the biblical Book of Esther, it is written (9:19–22) that the day should be celebrated with joy and feasting and the sending of presents of food to one another and gifts to the poor. While the joy and feasting are carried out by Jews the world around, the tradition of *shalah manot*, the sending of gifts, has largely lapsed.

Purim too is one of the festivals that has a special food. Actually it is a pastry called *hamantaschen*, that is, Haman's pockets. They are of dough topped with poppy seeds or some fruit paste, then pinched together into a three-cornered shape.

v

As the previous pages of this guide have tried to make clear, the Jewish festivals and holidays bespeak what might be called our theology of history. There remain two holy days through which we state our theology of "Man in the World," as it were. I refer to the New Year and the Day of Atonement.

Rosh Hashanah, literally "the head of the year," falls on the first day of the month of Tishri, seventh month of the Jewish calendar. That the beginning of the Jewish religious year should occur with the seventh month is not too strange when we remember that our school year may begin in September or our fiscal year in some other month. The number seven seems to have had a very special significance in Bible times. Thus, the seventh day, the seventh year (sabbatical), and the conclusion of seven cycles of seven years (jubilee). While the Jewish calendar for the lunar year does indeed begin in the spring, the event that dates the years is Rosh Hashanah.

Spiritually speaking, this is most appropriate since the first ten days of the month of Tishri, which Rosh Hashanah initiates and which *Yom Kippur*, the Day of Atonement, culminates, are a period of intense spiritual inventory. Known as the *Yomin Noraim*, Days of Awe, their purpose is to establish a regimen of reflective self-examination whose purpose is to bring the worshipper to the act of atonement.

These days have a special aura of spiritual awareness, with the evening worship introducing the Day of Atonement representing the highest level of sanctity in our calendar.

At home, the New Year is welcomed with a special service of sanctification at the table. After the blessing of candles, wine, and bread (traditionally a round loaf, probably indicating the cycle of time), there is a charming ceremony in which a slice of apple is dipped in honey and the following words are recited: "May it be your will, Lord God and God of our fathers, that you grant us a good year and a sweet one."

In the sanctuary, the New Year services, as well as those of the Day of Atonement, have evolved from the biblical commandments stated in Leviticus 23:23–32. The New Year, known to us as both the Day of Remembrance and the Day of Sounding the *Shofar* (ram's horn), still retains

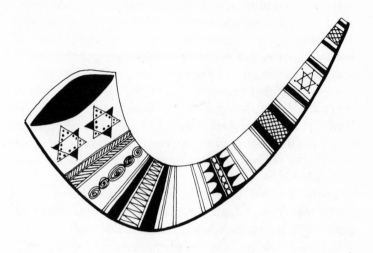

Ornamented Shofar (ram's horn)

as a central feature the blowing of the shofar. Even for one long accustomed to it, its sound has a commanding effect, with the power to alert the listener to the high solemnity of the occasion.

The service of worship and prayer prepares the individual for the deeply moving experience ten days hence when on the eve of Yom Kippur, the worshipper begins to seek forgiveness of God for his failings. Life is with people, as the saying goes, and sin is a wrong committed against a fellowman. Therefore it is expected that each individual try to achieve reconciliation with anyone whom he has wronged, prior to standing before God on the Day of Atonement. Reconciliation with man is antecedent to reconciliation with God.

The biblical source for Yom Kippur states three times that a man should afflict his soul on that day. Fasting from

evening to evening, which characterizes the Day of Atonement, is to be regarded only as a symbolic act, together
with other prohibitions that deny to the individual vain
self-indulgence. But neither formal religious requirements
nor the sheer length of the hours of worship can give the
sense of spiritual "presence" that the twenty-four hours
engender. From the opening chant of the *Kol Nidrei* (All
Vows) at the evening service to the blast of the shofar with
which the day is brought to an end, there is an atmosphere
that places the worshipper in the ambience of the holy.
Here is something "other."

Young and old alike are drawn into a mood of awe, a
mood that Yom Kippur, more than any other day, can
generate. It is, par excellence, *the* Holy Day.

It is a strange and moving phenomenon, the great rally-
ing of the people to synagogue and temple on the eve of
Kol Nidrei, the eve of Yom Kippur, and their awaiting the
chanting of words hallowed by tradition. What is it that
draws them? What is it that they hear? Few understand the
words of the Kol Nidrei, but all are spiritually responsive
to the mournful strains of its melody, which seems to
touch the raw nerve of the human condition. It is sad, but
not tragic, and in its conclusion it is affirmative and triumphant.

The theme throughout is forgiveness.

"May it therefore be Thy will, O Lord our God and God
of our fathers, to forgive us all our sins, to pardon all our
iniquities, and to grant us atonement for all our transgres-
sions." There follows a long catalogue of sins for which
forgiveness is sought: "For the sin which we have committed before Thee under compulsion or of our own free will
. . . unknowingly . . . openly or secretly . . . by wrong-
ing our neighbor . . . in commerce . . . in pride. . . ."

The old sense of corporate responsibility is there:

"We . . . us . . . our. . . ." No one person is guilty of all these sins, but all share in some way. The primal unspoken answer is there: "You are your brother's keeper."

Another theme of Yom Kippur is expressed through the *yizkor* (memorial) service. Although a comparable memorial service is included in the devotions for Passover, Shavuot, and Sukkot, none carries the sense of meaningfulness that the Day of Atonement elicits. In recalling to mind those who have been near and dear, as well as others whose death has been sacrificial on behalf of faith and people, Yom Kippur adds an extra dimension to ordinary remembrance. It is in the very nature of the day that the deeply moving questions of meaning and purpose in life are given priority.

The Day of Atonement comes to conclusion at day's end, with the prayer that the worshipper may be inscribed in the Book of Life, followed by a simple affirmation of faith: "Hear O Israel, the Lord our God, the Lord is One. Blessed be the name of his glorious kingdom forever and ever. The Eternal, He is God." The shofar is then sounded with a prolonged blast.

Following the sound of the shofar, the words "Next Year in Jerusalem!" are enunciated in Hebrew. The new Reform liturgy for the occasion translates them "Next year our people redeemed." The Ark, which had been opened for the concluding affirmation, is now closed, and the services are brought to an and. All are now ready for the break-fast, and exchange the holy day salutation: "Good *Yom Tov!*" (A good holy day) and *"Hatima Tovah!"* (May you be inscribed for good).

vi

Having listed and described our festivals (Passover, Shavuot, and Sukkot), holidays (Hanukkah and Purim), and holy days (Rosh HaShanah and Yom Kippur) in terms of their respective categories, it would, I believe, be helpful to place them in their time sequence through the calendar year. Passover leads the procession and is followed by Shavuot, the New Year and the Day of Atonement, Sukkot, Hanukkah, and, finally, Purim.

The Jewish reader will have wondered what happened to Simhat Torah and what place this guide will give to the Sabbath. Let him be at ease: This chapter concludes with a description of Simhat Torah; the Sabbath is explained in chapter 5.

Simhat Torah, rejoicing over the Torah, differs from all other festal days of the Jewish calendar. While it is, in a manner of speaking, the closing day of Sukkot, its connection with that festival's characteristics is nil.

It is with Simhat Torah that the cycle of weekly readings from the Pentateuch concludes and the new cycle begins. The ceremony engenders a great uplift of spirit, which indicates the extraordinary place that Torah has in the Jewish heart and mind. Traditional practice has all the scrolls of the Torah taken from the Ark and carried in sevenfold procession around the sanctuary. Reform custom may carry out this ritual in modified form.

The congregation is now ready to hear the reading of the concluding section of the Book of Deuteronomy (33:1–29), to be followed immediately thereafter by the reading of the opening section of the Book of Genesis.

The honor of reading the portion itself or the appropriate blessings pertaining thereto is highly regarded. Tra-

Torah with mantle and adornment

ditional and Reform practice may differ, but both involve elders and children alike in the joyful ceremony. The tradition of blessing the younger children with the words of Jacob (Gen. 48:16) while they stand under a *talit* (prayer shawl) finds its variant in the Reform use of Simhat Torah as occasion for blessing all children newly enrolled in the congregational religious school.

What is of special interest about Simhat Torah is that it, rather than Passover or the New Year, has become the annual occasion for thousands of young Jews in the Soviet Union to rally, as around a flag, for hours of song and dance in the square outside the great synagogue of Moscow. This use of the occasion represents an understanding—even though perhaps unconscious—of the central position of Torah in Jewish life. Although many, perhaps most, of the young people may be devoid of religious training, their annual Simhat Torah gathering is a kind of manifesto of their resistance to Soviet attempts to diminish Jewish religious and cultural life. In the Jewish calendar, every festival and holy day carries meaning; all say something about our understanding of the place of God in our personal or collective life. It is in Simhat Torah that the Jew celebrates more than the giving of the Torah; what is celebrated is the joy of study. When the great Hillel gave a thumbnail statement of Judaism's essential teaching as being to desist from doing to others that which is repugnant to ourselves, he concluded by saying "This is the teaching. Go now and study."

With Simhat Torah, we conclude the major events of the religious calendar. What has been listed does not exhaust the catalogue of occasions, some of which are marked by fasting, or introduce additional prayers into the prayerbook. It was not intended to do more than describe those religious events that, if only in small part, might be most commonly known to the average non-Jew.

But it should be known that new days of celebration and commemoration have been introduced into our liturgy, such as *Yom HaShoa* and *Yom Atzmaut* (pronounced Ahts-mah-oot), the first of which is Holocaust Day which commemorates the death of the six million Jews at Hitler's hands, and the second, Israel Independence Day. These have not yet taken on distinctive liturgical rites, but they have been increasingly widely marked by newly created prayers and, in some instances, by innovative services.

5

THE SABBATH

The idea of the Sabbath is Judaism's major contribution to Western religious thought, second only to the concept of monotheism. *Shabbat,* as it is known in Hebrew, finds the source of its observance in Genesis 2:3, "And God blessed the seventh day and declared it holy, because on it God had ceased from all the work of creation which he had done."

But mere cessation from labor does not explain the special spiritual dimension of the Sabbath. Exodus 31:17, after enjoining the Israelites to keep the Sabbath and to observe it as a covenant for all time, added these significant words: "For in six days the Lord made heaven and earth, and on the seventh day He ceased from work *and was refreshed"* (italics added). The Hebrew can be given a literal translation of "and was reinspirited," and, in truth, this is the spiritual goal that is sought in optimum observance of the Sabbath. The very special importance that the Sabbath had from earliest times is seen in the inclusion of its observance in the Ten Commandments.

The Sabbath has maintained its central place in Jewish religious life because, whether maximally or minimally observed, it holds within itself essential truths, the adherence to which has sustained the Jews throughout the millennia of their existence. It has been called an "island in time," a suspension of the tensions and efforts of the workaday world. But more than declaring man's right to periodic rest from labor, which puts the Sabbath into the category of being just a longer "time-out," the seventh day offers the Jew his chance to be reinspirited. The Sabbath is a manifesto of man's right to himself. It is a room of one's own, to which one can withdraw from the pressures of daily life and devote one's self to spiritual regeneration through meditation and study, and thus not only to prepare one's self for the week to come but even more to find one's place in relationship to time and eternity. The Sabbath reaffirms the need to maintain the line of separation between the holy and the mundane.

In order to maintain the sanctity of the day, there were developed over the centuries rules and guidelines dealing with what was and what was not appropriate for Sabbath activity. These rules evolved from biblical commandments respecting labor and use of fire on the Sabbath day (Exod. 20:8–11; 35:3). Thus, with regard to the latter, fire for keeping precooked food hot for the Sabbath was permissible, providing it was kindled prior to the Sabbath. However, for the duration of the Sabbath, the fire could not be attended to. The same principle would apply to illumination for the home.

But while there is considerable difference in the degree of observance of the Sabbath day by Jews in the spectrum from Orthodox to Reform, there is consensus as to the centricity of the Sabbath.

In Jewish tradition, Sabbath observance never carried overtones associated with "blue laws." The day was welcomed with joy as befits a festive occasion. Friday evening, the eve of the Sabbath, still sees families assembled around a table marked by special attention to its setting. Weekday clothes and appointments give way to a decor more befitting an hour that welcomes the "Sabbath Queen," imagery long used in Sabbath liturgy to describe the day.

In the home, the Sabbath is distinguished by a ritual that separates it from all other days of the week, the *Kiddush* (Sanctification). The blessing of candles, wine, and bread gives to the occasion an aura of spiritual beauty and peace. The traditional braided loaf, known in Hebrew as the *hallah*, recalls the manna, the "bread from heaven," that was gathered in double portion on the sixth day so that the people need not labor to gather it on the Sabbath (Exod. 16:22–29).

In the text of the Kiddush, the dual theme of the Sabbath is stated: It is at one and the same time a memorial to the creation and to the Exodus from Egypt. At the creation, man was endowed with soul; through the Sabbath, the soul finds liberation comparable to the liberation of the people of Israel from the Egyptian bondage.

In synagogue and temple, the Sabbath is marked by evening and morning worship services, the principal one of which occurs on Saturday morning and is the occasion for reading of the weekly portion of the Torah.

The Sabbath day comes to an end on Saturday night, when darkness has fallen. The conclusion is marked by a ceremony called *Havdalah*, separation, the moving beauty of which has often elicited comment from all who practice or share in its observance. The elements of the ritual include the kindling of a braided candle, the smelling of spices (usually placed in a decorative container), and the drinking of a cup of wine. The symbolism of candle and fragrant spices is colorful. The candle could not of course

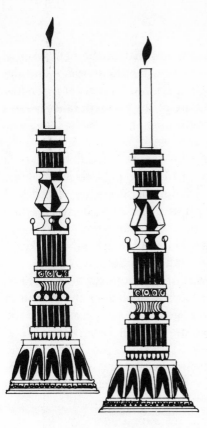

Sabbath candlesticks

Kiddush cup

be lit on the Sabbath; as the first act of the new week it parallels God's first act after creating the world—when he said "Let there be light!" Since the Sabbath gives to the Jew an "extra soul," the departure of the Sabbath takes the extra soul with it. The sweet pungency of the spices gives strength to the spiritually weakened Jew.

When the cup of wine is lifted, the Havdalah prayer is recited: "Blessed art Thou, O Lord our God, King of the universe, who makes a division between the sacred and the mundane, between light and darkness, between Israel and other nations, between the seventh day and the six working days. Praised be Thou, O Lord, who makes a separation between the sacred and the secular."

It has become a heartwarming custom for all present at the Havdalah to lock arms at its conclusion and to join in singing *"Shavua' Tov,"* a good week! Sometimes the words are sung in Yiddish as well: *"A Gute Woch."* The Sabbath, the weekly rededication of the Jew to basic teachings of his faith through home and sanctuary services, has concluded. The Sabbath Queen has departed, not to return until the following Sabbath.

6

THE WHERE AND HOW
OF PUBLIC WORSHIP

It is customary for the Jew to refer to his place of worship as either synagogue or temple—never church. Temple is more modern usage, and is generally applied to Conservative and Reform sanctuaries; *synagogue* is more often applied to Orthodox places of public prayer. Since the original Hebrew designation for the place where public prayer was held was *Bayt K'nesset*, house of assembly, for which the Greek translation is synagogue, this descriptive word has the validation of historic applicability. As a matter of fact, some congregations have reverted to the original sense of Bayt K'nesset, meeting place, by adding to their name the words *Jewish Center*—for example, "Congregation Shalom Jewish Center." But all Jewish congregations share the same objectives, no matter by what name they choose to be called: the offering of leadership and facilities for prayer, education, and social activities, as well as for whatever community needs require for the strengthening and perpetuation of Jewish life.

The Jewish house of worship is not distinguished by any particular architectural style. The medieval cathedrals usually had a cruciform ground plan; Protestant churches

are almost always topped by a steeple. However, just as
Christian churches often adorn the outside of their sanctuary building with a cross, so many synagogues and temples affix to the outside of the edifice such symbols as a
shield of David (six-pointed star), or menorah (seven-light
candelabrum), or burning bush.

If possible, the ground plan of the sanctuary interior
is laid out on an east-west axis, with seats so arranged that the worshipper faces east—that is, toward
Jerusalem. Orthodox practice does not allow men and
women to sit together; a separate section is reserved for
women. Conservative and Reform congregations provide
mixed seating, generally referred to as "family seating."

It should not be expected that the contemporary syna-
gogue/temple resembles the portable Sanctuary of the wilderness, described in Exodus 25 and successive chapters.
However, a few key elements of the biblical sanctuary
have survived as indispensable parts of the Jewish house of
worship. Thus the Holy Ark, which in biblical times held
"the Testimony" (Exod. 25:16; 1 Kings 8:9), is in the modern synagogue/temple a cabinet in which are placed the
Torah scrolls. In addition, there is the *parohet* (curtain):
"And the veil shall divide between the holy place and the
most holy" (Exod. 25:31, 33), and the *ner tamid* (eternal
light), to which reference is made in Exodus 27:20, 21. The
eternal light is so placed as to be visible whether the curtain is open or closed. The curtain itself may hang either
inside or outside the doors of the Ark. In addition to these,
in many sanctuaries, perhaps most, there is placed on the
dais a seven-branched candelabrum.

One ornaments what one loves and respects. The Jewish
sanctuary is no exception to this human tendency. The artistic enhancement of the religious accessories of the place
of worship or of the vestibule leading into the sanctuary is

Ark and curtain

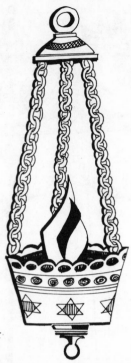

Eternal light over Ark

undertaken to heighten the mood of reverence. For readers, who may not have opportunity to see such contemporary artistic creations, I recommend *Contemporary Synagogue Art*, by Avram Kampf.

When the doors and curtain of the Ark are opened, one is able to see the mantled and adorned Torah scrolls, of which congregations will have as many as the generosity of donors makes possible. Not all Torahs are adorned in the same way, but all are covered with mantles of fabric whose color and ornamentation vary. While it is not mandatory to do so, many *Torot* (plural of Torah) will have beautiful silver ornaments atop the handles on which the Torah is rolled, usually in the shape of a crown. In addition, there may be a shield or breastplate hanging from the rollers, whose design may vary from traditional to quite contemporary. Finally, there will hang from the rollers a pointer (*yad*), which the reader of the Torah employs as he follows the words in order not to touch the parchment with his finger.

The overall effect is almost literally regal and majestic. One has the feeling that here is majesty in residence, with the ruler robed and sometimes crowned in a manner befitting his station. The place where he resides is, whenever possible, built of the finest materials and decorated in a way appropriate to the reverence with which he is regarded. When he comes forth to instruct and to counsel, all rise and remain standing until he is "seated." In fact, this image of Torah as king is further strengthened by the ritual practice at Simhat Torah when, immediately upon completion of the closing section of the Book of Deuteronomy, the first section of the Torah, Genesis, is begun anew. One is reminded of the cry raised when a king dies: "The King is dead; long live the King!" The second king is of course the dynastic or other successor king, and the manner of proclamation implies that between the old and the new there must not be even a moment of interregnum—not a moment when the land is without a ruler.

The figures of speech here employed are very close to exact description of the manner in which the Torah is regarded. The Torah is God speaking to man. The sense of place and of time past and present are intensified by the lines of tradition that move eastward toward Israel's beginnings. There are some temples and synagogues that are not thus oriented toward the east. But all share in the centricity of Ark and Torot, curtain and eternal light, just as the Christian church is oriented toward altar and cross.

The non-Jewish visitor who first attends a Jewish

worship service will observe a number of practices that distinguish the Jewish from the Christian service, or from Christian services in general. But the practices he observes will differ sharply depending on whether he is in a synagogue or temple. The adherence to such practices is the hallmark of the degree of traditionalism in the synagogue/temple. The essential differences between the traditional and the nontraditional congregation lie in the realm of ritual, custom, and ceremony, rather than in theology. Here, as always, the key question is: What modes of expressing the religious life are most conducive to the perpetuation of the Jewish faith and folk? Let it be noted, finally, that whether or not a custom is followed or not followed may be mandatory or permissive, depending on the point of view of the congregation.

Thus, the Jew traditionally wears a head covering (mostly referred to as a *yarmulke*) when he is at prayer. It is a custom whose origins are unknown but which has taken on the strength of religious law. In the synagogue it is required; in the Reform temple it is not required—the worshipper may wear it or not as he chooses, but for the most part the yarmulke is not worn.

The same principle applies to the wearing of the *talit*, prayer shawl. Whatever may have been its shape in biblical times, it has taken on the form of a wide stole whose ends are adorned with fringes, and to the four corners of which are attached slender tassels, in fulfillment of the law stated in Numbers 15:38–41. The purpose of the tassels (*tzitzit*) is "to ensure that you remember all My commands and obey them, and keep yourselves holy, consecrated to your God." The talit is often beautifully ornamented at the corners and neckband with gold or silver threads. Stripes of purple-blue or black run transverse to the width of the talit at its end. It is not customary for women to wear it.

Yarmulke and talit

The traditional synagogue has no hymnology, as Christian worship does, nor does the Conservative. The Reform movement developed a hymn book, but the singing of hymns by the congregation is not an integral part of the service, as it is in Protestant Christianity.

The historic source of music in the synagogue is the *hazzan* (cantor), whose primary role is to chant or sing the prayers. While his skills may be notable, his position within the framework of the congregation is secondary to that of the rabbi, who, through learning and spiritual stature, is the true leader of the congregation. Not all congregations can afford to employ a cantor. Guided by rabbi or reader, their worship is intermittently graced with the singing of liturgical passages whose melody has come down to them from earlier years. In the contemporary synagogue and temple, the hazzan doubles as religious educator and is responsible for preparing children for bar or bat mitzvah. Today, Reform congregations also employ a hazzan if they have the means to do so. The rabbi's role in the service will vary from that of reader/leader, with the cantor as assistant, to leader of the entire service. His principal task is to preach. By and large, the division of labor between rabbi and cantor is decided by mutual arrangement.

Choirs, as they exist in the Christian church, are principally to be found in Reform congregations. Whether their personnel is made up of members alone, or of paid professionals, varies from temple to temple. This does not mean that there are no choral groups in the more traditional congregations, but it is unlikely that they will have paid professional personnel.

Instrumental music, whether organ, piano, or other, has not been heard in the traditional synagogue since the destruction of the Holy Temple in Jerusalem. Whether it has place in the Conservative synagogue is largely a matter of "advise and consent" between rabbi and congregation. But it has had wide acceptance in the Reform service ever since the origin of the movement.

Although the Sabbath morning worship ranks as the most important of the week, since fixed selections from the Pentateuch and an accompanying biblical text are read at that time, there are regular weekday services as well. In traditional practice, the full service cannot be read without the presence of a quorum (minyan) of ten men. Reform Judaism has long abandoned the need for the quorum and, in addition, where the sense of legitimacy of the quorum survives, has accepted the principle of inclusion of women as members of the minyan. At the time this guide was written, the Conservative movement was debating the issue of the same inclusion. The legitimation of the participation of women in the public worship service includes privileges that run from acting as aides in the reading of the weekly Torah selection to actual occupancy of the pulpit as rabbis. Reform has already accepted the idea of women as rabbis, in both principle and practice. It seems reasonable to conjecture that full religious rights will be accorded women in all branches of American Judaism, save the most Orthodox, in the immediate future.

There is considerable difference among the prayerbooks of the various branches of Judaism. The differences are to be listed in terms of whether the *siddur* (order of prayer) is entirely in Hebrew or in both Hebrew and English, whether the prayerbook has been substantially edited to remove duplications of statement and/or of ideas found unacceptable to respective branches of Judaism, and whether the translations of the original Hebrew are simply paraphrases or even innovative writing in the spirit of the original. Thus, the Reconstructionist prayerbook omits all references to the doctrine of the Chosen People; the new Reform prayerbook makes use of paraphrases and innovative liturgy alike.

Another feature that distinguishes the Jewish worship is the fact that, save for a very few prayers, the wording bespeaks the adoration, hope, and petition of the group rather than of the individual: "Our God and God of our fathers"; "We beseech Thee, O Lord our God"; "Have mercy upon us"; "Enlighten our eyes in Thy Torah." The prayers of the Jewish people reflect our historic group consciousness. But the prayerbook reveals more than this: It mirrors the totality of Jewish thought. Prayer, therefore, becomes more than a reaching out to God; it is a daily and weekly restatement of the fundamentals of our faith, charged with the awareness that, in our worship, we are in intimate touch with time and eternity.

7

THE JEWISH HOME

Even before one enters the home, there is visible evidence that it is the home of a Jew. Long ago it was written (Deut. 6:9): "Write them [the Ten Commandments] on the doorports of your houses and on your gates." Out of this injunction there grew the custom of affixing to the doorpost of the home a container, called a *mezuzah,* in which was placed a scroll with the words from Deuteronomy 6:4–9 and 11:13–21 written thereon. On the reverse side of the scroll is inscribed the word *Shaddai* (Shahdye), the Hebrew name for God as Almighty.

The mezuzah thus has a threefold level of meaning: as reminder of God's law for man's moral conduct, as sign of God's protection, and as witness to the Jewish identity of the home's occupants.

The materials out of which the mezuzah is made vary, and the scroll itself may be either handwritten on parchment, as tradition calls for, or photocopied on paper, as modern technology has made increasingly common. The first letter of God's name, Shaddai, written on the back of the scrolls, may be made visible through a small aperture in the front of the mezuzah, or, lacking such an opening,

Mezuzah

the letter (*Shin*) may be designed into the face of the mezuzah.

What distinguishes the interior of the Jewish home? What visible signs of Jewishness? One can perhaps point to the Sabbath candlesticks or the nine-light Hanukkiah candelabrum or a Kiddush cup. Increasingly, one may see decorative placques or hangings with Jewish themes (Torah scroll, tree of life, burning bush), or perhaps mementoes or arts and crafts creations from Israel. But these latter have less reference to faith than to folk, even though the connection is somewhat tenuous.

It is at the table that one comes much closer to the atmosphere and practices that satisfy the deeper meaning of the word *religion*. The more observant the home, the greater the probability that Sabbath and festivals will find recognition when the family assembles for their celebration. But even at the most ordinary meal, it is traditional for the head of the house, or someone acting in his stead, to bless the bread before eating. The Jew "returns thanks" with this statement: "Praised art Thou, O Lord, King of the Universe, Who brings forth bread from the earth." We do not make spontaneous or other "invocations." That does not mean to say that there cannot be such, but simply that it is not Jewish custom.

Adherence to the practice of wearing the yarmulke while reciting blessings, whether before or after the meal, is a measure of the extent to which the participant regards himself as traditional or liberal.

Far more critical to religious practice in the home, as understood by the traditional Jew, is the observance of the dietary laws (*kashrut*, pronounced kahsh-root). Perhaps more than any other law of religious practice, kashrut has engendered the widest possible range of "variations on a theme." The Orthodox Jew and a great many Conservatives are scrupulously attentive to the demands of "keeping kosher" at home and outside the home. But there is an even larger number of Jews who comply with the laws of kashrut in only a "more or less" manner. And there are large numbers of Jews who are indifferent to its requirements.

It is the purpose of this guide to give sufficient clarification, so that the non-Jewish reader can understand the basis of traditional practice, while at the same time he is aware that such practices are not universal in the Jewish home, and even when observed in the home may be neglected when eating in public. The exigencies of modern life have done much to erode attitudes toward traditional laws, and so also have intellectual positions.

There are two basic areas of concern: forbidden foods and the mixing of dairy and meat foods. Leviticus 11 and Deuteronomy 14:2–21 list animals, fish, and fowl that one is permitted to eat and those that are prohibited. These two biblical sources validate laws that relate to permitted and forbidden foods. Three biblical verses are the source for laws that relate to the mixing of dairy and meat foods: Exodus 23:19, 34:26 and Deuteronomy 14:21. One other biblical law critically affects kashrut: Leviticus 7:26–27; 17:10–14.

In sum, meat to be *kosher* (ritually fit) must come only of animals, fish, and fowl in categories established by biblical law, must be slaughtered by knowledgeable experts who meet Jewish religious requirements, and, save for fish, must be free of blood.

The prohibition against mixing meat and dairy foods is, as noted above, based upon the injunction "You shall not boil a kid in its mother's milk." Whatever that law may have meant in biblical times, it has been rabbinically interpreted in a highly specific way. Not only may meat and dairy products not be eaten at the same meal, or within specified time lapses, but there must be a separate set of dishes for each category, unless the dishes used are of a material, such as glass, that is deemed not likely to retain vestiges of food after washing.

The extent to which such separation of utensils may go—as for example in the case of washing machines, sinks, and refrigerators—will depend upon the scrupulosity of the household, coupled with the guiding opinion of rabbinic authorities.

Because the purpose of this guide is both to describe and to interpret for the benefit of the non-Jew, a closing word is in order about the rationale of kashrut, as understood by the traditional Jew. The following quotation is from Hayim Halevy Donin's book, *To Be a Jew*. Rabbi Donin is Orthodox.

> The Jewish dietary laws prescribe not merely a diet for the body but a diet for the soul as well; not so much a diet to maintain one's physical well-being as a

diet to maintain one's spiritual well-being. . . . The only hint or clue that the Biblical text itself provides as to the reason for these regulations is that in almost every instance where the food laws are referred to in the Torah, we find a call to holiness. . . . Holiness meant and means becoming master over one's passions so that one is in command and control of them, and not they of him . . . there is no denying the inherent value in a religious discipline intended to train one to resist bodily drives and urges just to satisfy a craving or experience a pleasure . . . Kashrut is a good example of how Judaism raises even the most mundane of acts, the most routine activities, into a religious experience.

The Reform movement declared itself on the same subject in 1885 when, as part of its platform, it stated, "We hold that all such Mosaic and rabbinical laws as regulate diet, priestly purity and dress originated in ages and under the influence of ideas . . . entirely foreign to our present mental and spiritual state." Kashrut, accordingly, is not of prime concern to individuals who put themselves in the category of "liberal."

Special attention has been given to the dietary laws because there has been growing awareness of, and sensitivity to, the question on the part of Christians who do not wish to embarrass their Jewish guests at public or private meals—a thoughtfulness well appreciated by those Jews who periodically break bread with their Christian friends, and who are observant, if only in part, of religious dietary requirements. It is never amiss to ask a Jewish guest whether there is any food that is not on his diet. As a matter of fact, in these days of food facts, fads, and fancies, the question would not be amiss for any guest.

8
THE JEWISH CYCLE
OF LIFE

The way stations of human life, from birth to death, are universally accorded special custom and celebration. But it should be understood by the non-Jew—especially the Christian—that Jewish rites and ceremonies are not sacraments, if by sacrament is understood either a rite possessing a divine power inherent in itself or simply a channel of God's grace.

What are these way stations? Naming, circumcision, bar and bat mitzvah, betrothal, marriage, and death. For some there is the *Pidyon Ha-Ben* following circumcision.

In the following pages, this guide will attempt to describe the manner in which Jewish practice, both traditional and liberal, observes these milestones from life's beginning to its conclusion.

NAMING. It is in the naming that the child receives first identity. A boy is given his name at the time he is circumcised; a girl when her father, a week following her birth, is called to the synagogue rostrum when the Torah is read and a prayer recited for the good health of mother and newborn daughter. Although the ceremony may differ from congregation to congregation, it is a practice that has probably found general approval by most Rabbis and their congregations. The practice of publicly naming the girl-child implies a community recognition of the new life.

As with the infant boy, the girl is given a Hebrew name, very often one that borrows all or part of the name of a deceased and esteemed member of the family, although this is not necessary. It is not general Jewish practice to name a child after a person who is still living—particularly a living member of the family—although there is a segment of both traditional and Reform Jews who do so. For the most part, however, it is unlikely that a Jewish boy will have appended to his name either "Jr." or a numerical designation such as "III."

CIRCUMCISION. In traditional Jewish practice, every newborn son is circumcised on the eighth day after birth, by a mohel, a professional and trained circumciser, who at the time of the act gives the child his Jewish name, which may be in either Hebrew or Yiddish.

The injunction to circumcise the male child is clear and solemn: "This is how you shall keep my covenant between myself and you and your descendants after you. Every male among you in every generation shall be circumcized on the eighth day" (Gen. 17:10–14).

The act of circumcision is therefore clearly an act of covenant and not a sacrament comparable to baptism. It is a folk rite. As a matter of fact, it is known in Hebrew as *Brit Milah*, the covenant of circumcision. In that covenant rite, the father states, "Blessed art thou, O Lord, our God, King of the universe, who has sanctified us with his commandments, and commanded us to bring him [the son] into the covenant of Abraham our father."

Whenever possible, ten males above the age of thirteen

are witness to the event, as a traditional religious quorum. After the circumcision, there is a festive repast for family and friends, with many a *Mazal Tov!* (Good Luck!, but more essentially the traditional Jewish congratulatory expression) to father, mother, and whatever members of their respective families are present. Like other Jewish life-cycle occasions, the circumcision brings families together in happy celebration.

Deviations from the norm of eighth day circumcision by the mohel should be recognized as being just that. The concerned Jew will make every effort to hold to the traditional eighth day. But because it is not always possible to obtain the services of a mohel, or because the parents may not wish to do so, and, in addition, because there are Jewish parents who are indifferent to the eighth day requirement, variations on the practice have been devised. In some cases the child is circumcised before the eighth day, while the mother is still in the hospital. With a Jewish doctor performing the surgery and a rabbi as officiant, the circumcision becomes a Jewish ritual rather than a routine procedure. In other instances, the child may be circumcised at home on the eighth day, with rabbi and physician functioning as a team.

PIDYON HA-BEN (Redemption of the First-Born Son). As a demonstration of the persistence of custom, few if any traditions offer better example than the Pidyon Ha-Ben. As the guide has by now amply shown, the sense of what is religiously obligatory will vary according to the person's place in the spectrum of religious conviction. Nonetheless, this ritual, which the traditional Jew regards as a "must," is at the same time often a matter of concern even for individuals who regard themselves as liberal and who may have no understanding at all of its meaning. The reason is bound up with the nature of the human being. The experience of this author has been that in virtually all events related to the life cycle, people are concerned to do "the right thing." No matter how intellectualized their approach to all other traditional law and custom may be, in these matters there seems to be a built-in determination not to go against ancient procedures.

Why the Redemption of the First-Born? The ceremony is based upon three biblical laws: that the first-born son belongs to God, that the Levite can serve in place of the first-born (Num. 8:8, 14, 18), and that such redemption is betokened by payment of five shekels of silver (Num. 18:15).

Biblical law, extending through the ages into modern times, calls for the rite of redemption to take place at the "end of one month." The money is paid to a Jew whose rank is that of priestly class (*kohen*), who asks the father, "Which do you prefer: to give me your son or to redeem him?" Appropriate blessings are recited, and the father then gives five dollars or other silver coins to the kohen. After a few traditional words, the kohen recites the priestly benediction and then concludes the ceremony with blessing over a goblet of wine.

The ritual as described or witnessed may elicit some questions on the part of the non-Jew. Is the word *kohen* related to the omnipresent name Cohen or its variant forms (Cohn, Kahn, Cahn, etc.), or, what is the priestly blessing? A brief digression from our description of the Jewish life cycle will not be amiss.

The ancient biblical categories of priest and Levite carried with them important religious responsibilities. Subsequent generations of Jews traced their ancestry to these biblical Temple servitors, a genealogy that was noted by the use of the name Cohen or Levy, respectively.

The priestly benediction is probably well-known to the average Christian: "May the Lord bless you and watch over you; May the Lord's radiance shine on you; May he be gracious unto you; May the Lord lift up His countenance upon you and give you peace" (Num. 6:24–26).

BAR AND BAT (BAHT) MITZVAH. The meaning of *bar mitzvah* is "subject to [religious] law." It refers to a boy who, having reached the age of thirteen, is accounted old enough for both the responsibilities and the privileges of Jewish religious practice. Thus, he is expected to don the *tefillin* (phylacteries) for morning prayers and to fast on Yom Kippur and other fast days. At the same time, he is privileged to be included in the quorum of Services, as well as to be called up to recite the blessings associated with the reading of the Torah. In short, in the eyes of Jewish law, he has achieved his religious majority and may take his place with all adults in matters of religious obligation.

At its most minimal, the ceremony of bar mitzvah calls for the candidate to be called to the lectern at the time of the reading of the scrolls of the Torah, there to recite the blessings before and after its reading. In both Conservative and Reform practice alike, there has developed the procedure of having the bar and bat mitzvah candidate read all or part of the worship service, a part of the weekly Torah portion, and a section of the *Haphtorah* (associated readings from later biblical writings). In addition, there is likely to be the presentation of an address by the bar or bat mitzvah child.

Bat mitzvah really has no standing in Jewish law comparable to bar mitzvah, since the woman was traditionally never accorded the religious responsibilities and privileges given the man. However, the ceremony of bat mitzvah has taken a firm hold in modern American Jewish practice as a "coming of age" rite, representing as it does the growing tendency to recognize the validity of including women in the full religious life of the congregation. Obviously, that inclusion will vary according to the firmness with which the congregation holds to traditional ways.

The rituals of bar and bat mitzvah alike vary considerably in the extent to which the boy or girl participates in the service of the Sabbath eve or morning on which the event occurs, and at the same time mirrors the extent of preparation required. However that may be, the most obvious fact about the bar/bat mitzvah event is the high degree of importance given it by the parents and family of the—now—young man and woman. It is an occasion for gathering from far and near, for gift-giving and festivity, as though family and community alike were celebrating a major occasion. And it is such, since it combines the life-frontier-crossing of becoming a teen-ager with religious and folk significance. That is why, although the custom was for a very long time discarded by the Reform movement, sharper insights into the deeper values of bar mitzvah brought it back into the calendar of its life-cycle ceremonies—and bat mitzvah followed in due course.

CONFIRMATION. In its beginnings, confirmation was a Reform substitute for bar mitzvah, and, unwittingly anticipating later custom, for bat mitzvah as well. Taking the name of the Christian practice, but without its theological meaning, and coupling it with Jewish tradition, confirmation was a Reform version of a coming-of-age ritual, a ceremony of dedication.

At the same time that bar mitzvah began once more to take hold, confirmation began to lose its character as life-cycle event. Little by little, the age level for confirmation advanced until it became an occasion not unlike high school commencement exercises. Today the average age for confirmation is about sixteen or seventeen. Some Jewish leaders and educators believe that the designation "confirmation" should give way to a different one—perhaps "affirmation"—since confirmation has Christian associations that have no relationship to the Jewish interpretation of what confirmation should mean to the young Jew.

All in all, confirmation/affirmation today is much closer to being a leave-taking ceremony at the conclusion of upper or high school levels of Jewish education under the roof of the congregation than it is a strictly life-cycle ritual.

BETROTHAL AND MARRIAGE. Behind the simplicity of the marriage ceremony lie the complex lines of history and custom, coupled with the wealth of meaning that Jewish thought has bestowed upon the occasion.

Unlike other milestones in the life cycle, marriage alone generates new life cycles. If only for that reason, it is a human experience of the utmost importance. The traditional Jewish marriage ceremony combines a sense of sanctity with the practicalities designed to make the marriage sound and stable.

Although they are not immediately apparent, the ceremony incorporates two elements: betrothal and marriage. In a more ancient day, the two were separated by varying lengths of time, but custom and necessity have brought them together into one ritual. One symbolic element that had its beginnings in biblical times is the *huppah*, the canopy, which in its origins was the tent or marriage chamber in which consummation took place. The floral arch or canopy so common in most weddings today—including the Jewish—may owe its origin to comparable beginnings.

The essential elements of the traditional Jewish wedding are: the blessing over the ritual wine, the giving of the ring and the verbal statement that accompanies that act, the reading of the *ketubah* (marriage contract), and the recitation of the "seven blessings." The essential thought of each blessing follows, with the reader to understand that attendant upon each blessing are the characteristic Hebrew words with which the blessings begin: "Praised art Thou O Lord our God, King of the universe . . ." who creates the fruit of the vine; who created all things for his own glory; who is man's creator; who created man in his own image; who causes Zion to rejoice through her children; who causes groom and bride to rejoice; who is the source of all rejoicing and causes the groom to rejoice with his bride.

It is to be expected that there will be variation between Orthodox and more modern practice, but it is more in the relative place of ritual elements in the ceremony than in such critical elements as the wording employed in the ring exchange. The Orthodox text does not take a ring exchange into consideration; it is the man alone who bestows the ring. But whether traditional or liberal, all ceremonies include the essential statement for the groom: "Behold, you are consecrated to me with this ring, as my bride, according to the law of Moses and Israel." In an exchange of rings, the bride repeats the words (in both Hebrew and English) but substitutes the words "as my husband."

In liberal practice, there is still interest in using the huppah, as well as the breaking of a glass underfoot by the bridegroom. This custom is just that—a custom—and not an integral part of the service as such. It is an ancient custom that may have had its origins in that dim past when man sought to frighten away the evil spirits with noise. But the custom has long since been given a Jewish interpretation: that even in the midst of joyous celebration, one should recall the misfortune of the destruction of the Temple in Jerusalem—joy must be tempered with sobriety.

The ketubah requires a word of explanation. In its origins it was in fact a marriage contract, a legal document, not just a "certificate of marriage," whose phrasing brought together two elements in the marriage: (1) an affirmation that having taken the woman to be his wife, the groom will honor, work for, and maintain his bride "in accordance with the custom of Jewish husbands," and (2) as an aspect of that maintenance, the husband acknowledging the wife's dowry and adding thereto a portion of his own possessions, underwriting a lien on his possessions in the event that he divorce her without rabbinically legal cause.

The modernizing of the ketubah has in some instances kept much of the old wording in the original Aramaic language, but in its translation it has omitted outmoded contractual elements. Other ketubot have retained only as much of the original text as conforms to the contemporary idea of a certificate of marriage.

The retention of the title "ketubah" for certificate, even though it is no longer what it once was, is, of course, an effort to give the ceremony an additional Jewish character, whether the document is read during the course of the ceremony or simply given the newlywed couple afterwards.

One final comment about the Jewish marriage ceremony: Even when the contractual elements were present in every ritual of marriage, the deeper and truer nature of the act was denoted many times during the service. The words of the groom—and now of the bride as well—speak of consecration; the seven blessings are a sevenfold invocation of God's presence; at the beginning in the traditional service (and at the conclusion in the Reform ceremony), these words are recited: "Praised art Thou, O Lord, Who sanctifies His People Israel, through the Huppah and the sacred covenant of wedlock."

Obviously, a marriage has civil and legal implications, but in traditional Jewish law its dissolution must be rabbinically validated before another marriage can be entered into. More liberal practice recognizes civil divorce.

DEATH, BURIAL, MOURNING. More than any other phase of the life cycle, the laws and customs relating to death, burial, and mourning throw light upon Jewish thought with respect to the nature of man and, indeed, of human nature.

Before death, it is prohibited to leave the dying person unattended, lest he be alone when his soul takes leave of him. In every way it is made clear that the terminally ill person is not just another patient but a mortally sick human being whose going should be neither hastened nor impeded.

Even after death, both law and custom clearly indicate that the body is not just a corpse to be dealt with casually. Though it is lifeless, the dignity that attached to it when living still attaches to it. The very requirement to carry out the burial as soon as possible after death, save on the Sabbath or the first day of festivals, came into being because it was felt that to remain unburied is a dishonor to the dead. The least of men merits such care since, as tradition has it, "With what is death comparable? With the burning of a Scroll of the Torah, as there is none so worthless in Israel, who neither possessed some degree of knowledge, nor had fulfilled some of its commandments."

It was for that reason that all who were present at the

passing of the deceased were required to rend their garments in prescribed ways. This tradition of rending the garment has its modern equivalent in a symbolic tearing, wherein a small black ribbon, already torn, is affixed to the garment of the mourner as part of the funeral procedure. Orthodox tradition rejects this type of rending as being unacceptable.

Following death, the body of the deceased is prepared for burial by the *Hevra Kadisha* (Holy Brotherhood), a sort of committee of the congregation charged with the responsibility of after-death ritual requirements, such as washing the body and preparing it for burial. Not all congregations have such Hevras, but they are generally in existence wherever there is adherence to traditional practices. In addition to the ritual washing of the body, the deceased is traditionally clothed in white shrouds, and both *talit* (prayer shawl) and *yarmulke* (ritual head covering) are also put on the body. Although the wearing of shrouds is less and less practiced even by the more traditional, the use of talit and yarmulke or at least of the talit has become increasingly common.

Embalming is not part of Jewish tradition, since the blood is regarded as an integral part of the person and must therefore not be disposed of as waste. In a manner of speaking, we may regard this Jewish attitude as a rejection of violence against the body, even though it is lifeless; it is a reflection of concern for human dignity.

By the same token, autopsies were forbidden. More anciently rooted in the belief in resurrection, the body was to be buried whole, from which thought came the obligation to bury dismembered parts separately. In addition, there was the strong feeling that autopsy was an act of desecration. However, because furtherance of life takes precedence over all, autopsy was ultimately validated by rabbinic authority when it could be established that immediate benefit to others would ensue.

CREMATION. Although cremation is against traditional Jewish law, it is permitted in Reform practice, even though it is not generally encouraged. There are those who feel that a graveside burial visibly denotes return to the earth and the finality of separation.

THE CASKET. Jewish law requires that the casket be completely of wood (no nails or metal handles). Metal caskets and concrete burial vaults would retard the natural processes and are therefore not in keeping with Jewish law. Even where traditional Jewish law is not followed today, the tendency is to encourage the utmost simplicity and, as far as possible, to stay close to the spirit of traditional practices.

VIEWING THE REMAINS. Public viewing of the body, while not prohibited by any specific Jewish law, is discouraged in practice. It is sometimes the family's desire to view the body in privacy, prior to the funeral service, but to leave the casket open during the public services is discouraged as against traditional Jewish values relating to respect and honor for the dead.

THE FUNERAL SERVICES. The two principal liturgical elements of the burial service are the reciting of *El Molay Rahamim* and the *Kaddish*. The latter, which is traditionally a part of the service conducted at the home of the mourners prior to the funeral, has, in practice, become a part of the services conducted in the funeral chapel.

The text of the El Molay Rahamim implores God to grant pardon and rest under the shadow of his presence, to the soul of the departed. "Shelter him (her) under the cover of Thy wings, and let his (her) soul be bound up in the bond of eternal life. The Lord is his (her) inheritance, may he (she) rest in peace. And let us all say 'Amen.' "

The Kaddish is essentially a doxology, which, though it has no reference to death, has become the mourner's prayer, and in traditional practice it is recited by close male kin of the deceased. Reform practice, since it has a different position with respect to women and liturgy, makes no distinction between male and female mourners.

The service is begun in the chapel—where the El Molay Rahamim finds place in the liturgy—and concludes in the cemetery, where the Kaddish is recited by the mourners.

MOURNING. After the burial, the mourners and their friends return home. Although there are long-established differences between traditional and liberal observance of mourning customs, the common ground is broad enough to allow the observation that there is general agreement as to what is considered appropriate.

Jewish tradition associated with the bereaved home calls upon friends and neighbors to provide the "meal of condolence" on the first day of mourning. Needless to say, this practice is rarely confined to the first day. Prepared food brought to the house of mourning not only is a response to tradition but shows a sympathetic understanding of the need to lighten the household work of the mourners at a time when such routines become an inappropriate burden.

There are three well-defined periods of mourning. The first is known as *shiva* (seven) and refers to the seven-day period of mourning that begins immediately following burial. Shiva is observed for father, mother, wife or husband, son, daughter, brother, or sister. The characteristic practice of shiva includes sitting on stools or seats lower than normal height, and the avoidance of activities that reflect attention to the self, such as grooming of the hair, the beard, or the hands, or even the wearing of fresh garments: in short, any activities that are, in effect, self-indulgence.

During the shiva period, a seven-day memorial candle is kindled, and appropriate services recited. In Reform practice, it is not required to observe traditional shiva customs, but the holding of home services is encouraged.

The second period of mourning is known as *"sh'loshim,"* which means thirty, and refers to the thirty days following the end of shiva. The origin of the idea of sh'loshim is probably Deuteronomy 34:8, where it is recounted that the Israelites mourned Moses' death for thirty days. Jewish tradition discourages joyful acts such as parties or weddings during this period. Reform Judaism does not have such specific prohibitions but recognizes the propriety of traditional practice. Sh'loshim concludes all mourning for close kin except for father and mother.

The final period of mourning, *avaylut,* which simply means "mourning" (for father or mother) terminates at the end of eleven months from the day of death. Traditional practice avoids pleasurable occasions of all types. Wherever a congregational quorum is available for that purpose, the mourner recites the Kaddish daily; in Reform Jewish practice, such recitation may be at weekly Sabbath services if daily services are not available.

Thereafter, the Kaddish is recited each year on the anniversary of the day of death. This occasion is known as the *yahrzeit,* which has the literal meaning of "anniversary." Traditional usage will observe the yahrzeit according to the day on which death occurred in the Jewish religious calendar; Reform usage allows for the use of the civil calendar. The yahrzeit begins with the evening preceding the date of death and is customarily marked with the lighting of a twenty-four-hour memorial candle.

MEMORIAL STONE. The putting up of a monument or the laying of a headstone can take place any time after the first month of mourning, and before the yahrzeit. Custom usually has the dedication by the eleventh month. By having the unveiling at the end of the first month, the ceremony in effect marks the conclusion of the sh'loshim period of mourning.

9

THE JEWISH FOLK

Even where there are substantial differences in approach to the questions with which religion is concerned—the nature of God, or the place of man in the universe—Judaism and Christianity have enough in common to be able to speak to each other with a more or less common vocabulary. The Jewish faith can be readily discussed, even if not readily accepted by the faithful Christian.

It is when the discussion moves to the subject of the Jewish people that present-day Christians encounter difficulty, for there is no shared ground or historic experience. As a matter of fact, the situation is made more difficult by the fact that in our time, most, if not all, people are identified by nationality, by race or faith, or by general categories of political and economic alignment. But other than the Jew, what grouping of people manages to fit into all of these categories and yet transcend them all?

In terms of today's categories of population groupings or classifications, the Jew is regarded as something of an anomaly: He does not fit neatly into any one compartment. Underlying the diversity of his national, political, and even racial identification, there is the commonality of his identification as Jew, which somehow transcends, or is other than, these aforementioned identifications. In the previous section of this guide, effort was made to indicate that "Jew" or "Jewish" does not indicate a uniformity of belief and practice, save in a shared monotheism. But whatever the differences in those beliefs and practices, there is a shared identity, and that identity exists without being compromised by national, racial, or any other identification. A Jew may be French, Italian, South African by national origin or citizenship, be fair, swarthy, or even black (as in the case of Ethiopian Jews), and be of any political/economic philosophy whatsoever, but he is at the same time a Jew.

There is another, but not related, source of confusion about the modern Jew. The average Christian who has given any thought to the matter at all finds it difficult to relate the contemporary Jew to the biblical Hebrew or Israelite, or to the Jew whose existence is mirrored in the New Testament. There has been a long road since Jesus' generation. The thoughtful Christian asks, "What is the connection between this Jew whom I know as my neighbor and my friend and that vague creature I know as 'biblical man'? What happened in the intervening centuries? Is my contemporary still a 'biblical Jew,' and if so, how? If he is not, what is he?"

It is said that "good fences make good neighbors." But such fences are good because they are low enough for neighbors to talk across.

It is the intention of this section to talk across the fence, to answer the hypothetical questions asked above (not so hypothetical, since they are often asked), as well as a good many others, which, it is hoped, will throw light on the kind of way in which we live and meet our felt needs. Since, in order to do that, it is necessary to explain something about Jewish origins, the sense of collective identity, and how we came to be scattered across the world, it would probably be most useful to have a brief look at our origins. The guide's approach to the development of the sense of folk or peoplehood will be to assume that the biblical account, even where seemingly legendary, contains a core of historical accuracy. After all, folk memories are a very good index of what later generations preserved as actual historical experiences, and, most important, they are a register of those ideas about self through which the people interpret events of the present and make projections into the future. With this thought, we are prepared to venture into the story of the Jewish people as People, which will take us from Bible times into our own day.

i

If the covenant at Sinai is (rightly) regarded as the pivotal point of all later Jewish history, what is the meaning of the accounts that relate the history of Abraham, Isaac, and Jacob, whose wanderings are described in the chapters between Genesis 11 and the Book of Exodus? According to Genesis 12:2, God said to Abram, "I will make of you a great nation." But neither Abraham nor Isaac nor Jacob, who became the historic Fathers of the Jewish people, ever became more than groupings of families with their respective retinue and livestock. They did not constitute a people. Their role was to bear witness to Adonai as God, and to be living testimony to God's promise to create out of their descendants a great people resident on their own land. What happened before Moses and the Exodus from Egypt was the strengthening of a vision of the future, which would bind the God of Israel to the people of Israel and the land of Israel.

In modern times, there have been various references to Jews as "Hebrews" or "Israelites"; such designations have not been used by non-Jews alone. But the word *Hebrew* as it might be applied to a particular people is purely biblical in nature. The name seems to have been used "when foreigners are introduced as speaking . . . or where Israelites are represented as speaking of themselves to foreigners" (Gesenius *Lexicon*, entry *'Ivri*). Today, *Hebrew* is appropriate only when speaking of the language.

The biblical ancestors of the Jews thought of themselves as "Children of Israel." That is, they traced their ancestry to Jacob, whose alternate name, Israel, according to biblical account, was given him after his struggle with the divine Being, at the river Jabbok (Gen. 32:29). The twelve tribes of Israel were identified by the names of Jacob's sons. In folk memory they, together with their children, make up the clans, tribes, and families who were the Children of Israel.

The Israelites whom Moses led out of Egypt, while they shared a sense of common ancestry, were in no sense a people as they would be so designated by God at Sinai. It was there that the tribes, clans, and families were given the terms of a treaty, so to speak, through which, if they chose to accept it, they could advance from being the loosely structured children of Israel to becoming the people of Israel.

The words of promise and the people's response are so fraught with historic importance for the story we are tracing that they are worth quoting in full, for it is to their spirit that future leaders reverted again and again in the effort to give meaning to the people's existence.

Thus shall you say to the house of Jacob, and declare to the children of Israel: "You have seen what I did to the Egyptians, how I bore you on eagles' wings and brought you to Me. Now, then, if you will obey me faithfully and keep my covenant, you shall be my treasured possession among all the peoples. Indeed, all the earth is mine, but you shall be to Me a kingdom of priests and a holy nation." These are the words you shall speak to the children of Israel. Moses came and summoned the elders of the people, and put before them all the words that the Lord had commanded him. All the people answered as one, saying, "All that the Lord has spoken we will do." And Moses brought back the people's words to the Lord (Exod. 19:3–8).

This is the very essence of a covenant: The conditions were laid down, and they were accepted.

Of course, peoplehood is not the same as political unity. Our own country bears witness to this truth. Although we are bound together by the fact of our being Americans, the zealous protection of states' rights, coupled with regionalism, is often in disagreement with, if not in resistance to, "Washington."

In like manner, the Israelites. It took a long time before strong tribal differentiation and occasional alliances yielded to centralization of government. But even that did not last long. The country became divided into northern (Israel) and southern (Judah) kingdoms. But despite the tensions and hostilities that so often disrupted the rule of kings, there was the awareness of identity as one people, in covenant with YHWH/Elohim, and occupying the land that he had pledged to Abraham.

The groundwork for all subsequent Jewish history was laid in the biblical period. The folk understanding of what it meant to be the people of Israel in covenant with God is summed up in the excerpt from Exodus quoted above. All the evidence points to periodic deviation from the commitment made at Sinai; it was left to that extraordinary band of men, the prophets, constantly to hold—or try to hold—the people to their convenantal obligations. At the same time, they proclaimed new teachings about the nature of God and his role in the life of man.

After the prophets came the teachers, the scholars, the Rabbis. Between the era of Ezra and the destruction of Jerusalem by the Romans in 70 C.E., five centuries were to elapse. During those centuries it was as if a blade were honed against a whetstone. The blade was the Jewish nation, the stone the successive conquering nations—Greek and Roman—under whose sovereignty the abrasion of contact was both spiritual and physical. Self-rule was not independence. In the best of times, there was autonomy; in the worst of times, intrigue, civil war, and misrule, coupled with Roman intervention, led to the ultimate dissolution of that autonomy. In the end the dimension of resistance, with its violence and bloodshed, brought about harsh suppression by Rome. The cost in Jewish lives was massive, but the worst calamity was the destruction of the Temple in Jerusalem in 70 C.E., for the Temple was the Jewish world's spiritual center. It was the third major watershed of Jewish history.

Although decimated by war, there was still a Jewish population in Palestine/Judea, with a rabbinic leadership that sought to create new guidelines for Jewish life without the Temple. But the political spirit of the people called for renewed attempts to gain independence. The final uprising came in 134/135 C.E., under the charismatic leadership of Bar Kohba, but was brutally crushed. Jerusalem was renamed Aelia Capitolina, entry was prohibited to Jews, and all hope for Jewish independence came to an end.

ii

There was no longer a Jewish nation, but there was a Jewish people—scattered, to be sure, but intensively involved in the regrouping of its spiritual forces. Wherever such clustering of Jews was to be found, whether small or large—and they were to be found in virtually every land of the then known world—a process was going on that would consolidate their collective existence and pave the way for folk survival for many centuries to come.

The kinds of organizations or activities that came into being met the most pressing needs of the far-flung communities and exercised important influence on later Jewish life. It is worthwhile to describe them, even though in simplified form, for they help us to understand what is meant by "mechanisms of survival."

First, and surely foremost, was the synagogue. What was so radically important about the early synagogue was that it made possible the existence of a center, wherever the people were themselves situated. From the beginning (possibly in the days of the Babylonian exile of the sixth century B.C.E.), the synagogue was a place of assembly; indeed, that is the meaning of the word. Here was "town meeting hall," school, and archives, as well as locale for early efforts at formalized worship. Such worship was more than structured prayer into which new elements entered from time to time; it was itself an educational activity. One might refer to the synagogue as the spiritual mint in which was coined the currency of Jewish spiritual values. For with the reading of the Pentateuch, coupled with selections from other parts of the Scriptures, came sermonic interpretations that by their very nature emphasized ongoing values rooted in the past.

No matter where it may be, a community interacts

within itself and with the government of which it is a part. There must be leaders, spokesmen, legal authorities, representatives. There are the poor, the orphans, the widows. There are the merchants, the laborers, the transients. A community, to be coherent, to survive, and to prosper, must create rules and standards, have the power to tax itself for the benefit of its institutions.

The Jewish communities of the early centuries of this era shaped the prototypes of agencies that are still to be found in modern Jewish life.

In addition to the synagogue, which became predominantly a house of worship, there was great emphasis upon the importance of education for both children and adults. It was expected—indeed, required—that the education of children begin no later than their sixth year, and while such education was primarily the responsibility of the parents, provision was also made for communal education. Education was expected to go beyond mere literacy to knowledge of biblical and postbiblical literatures. Obviously, such education was for more than the purpose of knowing the "literature." The purpose of study was to sensitize mind and spirit to religious doctrine and practice. Not all became scholars, of course, but all were exposed to study, and the tradition of learning became increasingly deeply rooted in Jewish life.

Another concern, one that had biblical roots but for which new agencies were created, was the care of the needy. Biblical law saw to it that a portion of each man's harvest was left for the poor; this was an individual responsibility. But just as education of the child was both parental and communal, so provision for the destitute became communal as well as individual. Indeed, it was inevitable that in the cities where urban patterns made agricultural activities inoperative, such provision would have to be made. Under the circumstances, laws provided for both the collection and the distribution of funds and food. It is interesting to note that the idea of our modern "United Way" or Community Chest was already in effect in Jewish community life in the early centuries of the common era.

In short, the Jewish people, although widely dispersed from the ancient land, the original center of worship and focus of national identity, not only survived but, by creating communal agencies to meet all felt needs, actually intensified their collective identity.

Earlier, it was stated that the modern Jew could not be understood without some understanding of what took place in postbiblical times: the development of the rabbinic tradition and the ultimate creation of that vast compendium of Jewish law and lore called the Talmud. The Jewish communal patterns bear this out. For although the highly diversified character of the communities—depending on whether they were in the East or the West—made variations in custom inevitable, the overall similarities were due to the far-reaching influence and authority of rabbinic teaching.

In his important study, *The Jewish Community*, Salo W. Baron says:

> The enormous discrepancies in Jewish life were welded by the talmudic sages with remarkable finality into a common basic pattern, which was to last until the break-up of the Ghetto during the three centuries of the modern period. Centered in the hardly tangible synagogue of any ten adult males and the even less tangible *bet ha-midrash* (school) of students gathered around a recognized teacher, the Jewish community was eminently equipped for its subsequent struggle for survival under varying conditions

and in changing environments. . . . The recon-
structed communal organism acquired a vitality and
adaptability which stood it in good stead among all
civilizations which it was to encounter in its historic
career until the Industrial Revolution and the rise of
science. Not until then was the Pharisaic-rabbinic
doctrine and way of life discarded or even modified in
any essentials.

Agencies and organizations, social patterns, and communal leadership reflect the people's needs, folk values,
and traditional experiences. But they also reflect the exter-
nal world of the non-Jew. They reflect the laws under
which the Jewish communities lived, and the necessary interaction with prevailing governments. In the early centuries of the Diaspora, the Jewish people in their various
communal groupings enjoyed a good deal of acceptance.
Within the framework of the Roman Empire, they were,
with few exceptions, a tolerated "folk/faith." But all that
changed with the change in status of Christianity, which
occurred with the conversion of Emperor Constantine in
the fourth century. This account cannot properly proceed
without an understanding of the people's experience under
Christianity.

10
THE JEWISH PEOPLE AND CHRISTENDOM

Today's world is the product of all our yesterdays. To the same extent that the modes of organization of Jewish communities during those early centuries of the common era created patterns that were followed and enlarged upon in the centuries to come and are reflected in modern Jewish life, the attitudes and behavior of the early Christian church toward the Jews created patterns and precedents for those same subsequent centuries that, in like manner, are reflected in modern life.

We who live in a tradition where the separation of Church and State is written into our Constitution cannot perhaps fully realize what it means for the State to be fully subservient to the wishes of the Church, to make common cause with it for reasons ranging from the "religious" to the economic.

In his *History of the Jews Since the First Century A.D.*, Albert Schweitzer writes that the historian of the Jewish middle ages is "confronted with a reign of terror," and he explains this description with the following words:

> Theologians of the early patristic age were strongly conscious of the need to separate Christians and Jews.

Their efforts to do so were carried to drastic extremes, especially in the third century when the bonds between church and synagogue were sundered at last in a war of words. More and more insistence was made that Christians alone were heirs to the biblical promises, an inheritance which Jews had forfeited by their refusal to accept Jesus: furthermore, that His death had made them guilty of deicide; that as a people they were externally hateful to God; that no punishment or degradation was too extreme for them; that they were given over to devil worship; that they were a plague with whom Christians should not consort; that they were pariahs for whom there could be no salvation, etc., etc.

Here we have the roots of anti-Semitism. The Church, through its writings and preaching, could and did create a climate of attitude toward the Jew that made possible—and indeed, inevitable—the "reign of terror" of which Schweitzer spoke. Over the centuries, it was not constant, and there were periods of easement, but by and large Jewish life had to be carried on within the framework of events that ranged from exploitation to outright persecution, forced conversion, and exile.

Because this historic experience has played such a critical role in the life and development of the Jewish people, the reader should have some understanding of how the events referred to were spelled out.

As early as 315 C.E., the Roman Emperor Constantine gave Christianity a preferred position in his empire and at the same time threatened converts to Judaism with death by burning.

In 339, Constantius forbade marriages between Jewish men and Christian women "lest the Jews induce Christian women to share their shameful lives. If they do this, they [the Jewish husbands] will be subject to a sentence of death."

In 439, it was written into the Code of Theodosius that no new synagogues were to be built, that Jews were not to proselytize anyone, and whoever did so would lose both life and property.

In 531, Emperor Justinian ruled that "no heretic, nor even they who cherish the Jewish superstition, may offer testimony against orthodox Christians who are engaged in litigation. . . ."

In the seventh century, those Jews of Spain who, having been given the choice between baptism or expulsion, chose to be baptized were compelled to present a memorandum to the king in which they totally foreswore any reversion at all to their former Jewish practices on pain of being executed by stoning or burning. In the event such punishment for backsliding was set aside, the king had power to give the culprit slave status and to confiscate his property.

The conditions for the exploitation of the Jews were firmly established. Jews were fair game for rulers who could admit them or expel them for any reasons that seemed to them advantageous and proper, and in other ways exploit their potential for profit.

Thus, when the fifteen-year-old Philip Augustus came to the throne of France in 1179, he soon imprisoned all the Jews in his lands, then released them after receiving a very heavy ransom. In 1181 he annulled all loans made to Christians by Jews—while he took 20 percent for himself. The following year he drove all Jews out of the lands directly controlled by himself. Sixteen years later, he allowed Jews reentry into France but saw to it that their banking business became a source of profit to himself.

Throughout the Middle Ages the practice of using Jews

as sources of income, through special taxation, was an established procedure. As a matter of fact, the advantage of having Jewish banking and trade stabilized to the ultimate benefit of the country of their residence was attested to by a charter to the Jews of the Duchy of Austria in 1244, wherein every effort was made to protect the Jew against the misadventures, deceits, and vandalism to which his special status might make him vulnerable. Jacob R. Marcus, in his excellent source book, *The Jew in the Medieval World*, details a number of the provisions of the charter.

As for exile, the Jews of England were expelled from that land in 1290; the Jews of Spain in 1492. These do not stand alone in this melancholy roster of events but are among the better known. The reader is referred to *Jewish History Atlas* by Martin Gilbert, wherein he can see with the aid of excellently drawn maps the full range of persecutions and atrocities perpetrated against the Jews of both Eastern and Western Europe. There are recorded with respect to both time and place the tragic events of those dark centuries: the massacres of Jews in the Rhineland towns, by Crusaders who saw no reason to wait until reaching the Holy Land in order to slaughter the infidel; the restriction of their residence to limited quarters called ghettoes; the enforced wearing of special garments such as the pointed "Jew hat," with occasional additional identity signs such as a Star of David patch—and much more of the same sort. True, the story of Jewish life was not one of unmitigated torment, but over the centuries the record has been one of many-faceted assault on the person and the spirit of the Jew.

Throughout the centuries, then, the Jew was a sort of nonperson, a marginal man, to whom attached every conceivable sort of superstition and against whom violences were generated—for the most part by mobs responsive to the fanatical oratory of clerics who kept alive the hatred and fear of the Jew.

During those dark and ominous centuries, there was little of which the Jew was not felt to be capable. I recommend to the readers of this guide the study of Joshua Trachtenberg's, *The Devil and the Jews*, wherein he traces the story of superstitions about the Jew, which run the gamut from distorted folk fantasy to outright obscenity.

To live with such ignorance and outrageous superstition is of course possible, even though uncomfortable. But when the mentality that generates and accepts such superstition moves from belief to action, the results can be a true case in point for a "reign of terror." Thus, when in 1348 the Black Plague swept over Europe and destroyed a reported twenty-five million people, the rumor was spread that the plague was brought about through an international Jewish conspiracy. The result of such a rumor can be foreseen. Torture led to "confession" and wider incrimination, and before the plague had run its course, "thousands of Jews in at least two hundred towns and hamlets were butchered and burnt" (Jacob R. Marcus, *The Jew in the Medieval World*).

Not the least among the superstitions was one that held that Jews used Christian blood in the preparation of matzot for Passover. It is ironic that in the second century C.E. the church father, Tertullian, complained of ritual blood libels brought against the Christians! That such a belief about Jewish practice could find credence in the twelfth and thirteenth centuries can be understood. But it recurred in seventeenth-century Poland, in the eighteenth and nineteenth centuries in Russia, and as might have been expected, in twentieth-century Germany under the Nazis.

There is little point to adding more to the foregoing account. The purpose of its statement was to give the reader a general overview of the desperate circumstances under which for so long the Jewish people lived in Christian Europe.

Ultimately, the more blatant and violent anti-Jewish ideas were to diminish, save for the dark periods of modern Russian and German history. But they were possible because the seeds of the past had grown into the full flower of modern anti-Semitism. If the Jew stopped being a non-person, save in Russia and Germany, there still attached to him elsewhere the stigma of being "different" in ways that, in the popular mind, ranged from strange and stubborn (resistant to Christian proselytizing) to secretive and cunning.

The tradition of exclusion from the mainstream of national development found its expression in university quota systems, limitation of opportunity in important areas of business and industry, and other ways in which equality of opportunity was nonoperative. In the early history of the United States the right to hold office was impeded by restrictions against non-Protestants. It is a matter of record that as late as 1809 a Jew, Jacob Henry, who had been elected to the North Carolina state legislature, was challenged by an opponent as violating the state's constitution. It was not until about 1858 that this disability clause was removed from the state's constitution.

It was stated earlier that today's world is the product of all our yesterdays. In the end, the winds of change drove away the murky clouds of the early and later Middle Ages and, under the influence of radical changes in the character of both national and international life, made open association between Jew and Christian a larger possibility. And yet, there would be no point to the writing of this guide did the Jew still not have to be "explained" to his neighbor.

11
THE MODERN AMERICAN JEWISH COMMUNITY

i

The two previous chapters have attempted to indicate the roots of characteristic Jewish communal institutions, coupled with the conditions under which collective life had to be maintained from early and later Middle Ages up to that period of Western history marked by events and eras such as the rise of capitalism, the French revolution, and the Industrial Revolution. These latter national and international experiences marked the easement of restraints and special liabilities imposed upon the Jewish people and therefore made it possible for the Jew to share more fully in the intellectual, cultural, economic, and political life of his times. Except in Eastern Europe, he moved from marginality into the mainstream of national life. For Europe at large, there had been the Middle Ages and then the Renaissance as eras along the way to modernity. The Jew, however, knew only a Middle Ages—until the Age of Enlightenment liberated him.

Throughout the turmoil and intellectual ferment of the new day, communities continued to function as they had for many centuries. Thrown back on their own resources, they met the day-by-day needs in traditional manner, and counseled together when confronting new dangers. To the extent that their autonomy made it possible to do so, communities followed a course of self-regulation, guided by talmudic law as well as by the recommendations or rulings of recognized rabbinic authorities of their own time or earlier.

The Jewish community in the United States as it is currently structured has been responsive to various major influences: the traditional institutions of religion, education, and social welfare (the latter both local and overseas), subtle and overt anti-Semitism, Zionism/Israel, and general cultural. Under those categories there can be found a rather large number of organizations concerned with everything from fund-raising to hospitals and orphanages, from Societies of Jewish Students to Jewish Community Centers, from community relations to social action in the field of legislation.

It is unnecessary to introduce the reader to each and every one of what can only seem to be a bewildering array of organizations. Should he wish to study the roster, he can best begin by turning to *The American Jewish Year Book*, an annual compendium of essays, statistics, listings, and general information, published in Philadelphia by the American Jewish Committee and the Jewish Publication Society of America.

The purposes of this guide will be better served by describing the ways in which the American Jewish community functions to meet its major felt needs, particularly to the extent that the average non-Jew becomes at least passingly aware of such functions and may therefore entertain some curiosity about them.

ii

To speak of the Jews of the United States as "the American Jewish community" is to do no more than to provide a handy expression for discussion and description. In a legal/corporate sense there is no American Jewish community. But legal/corporate sense or not, it is obvious that there are many Jews in the United States, and that the commonality of their shared interests and concerns entitles them to be known as the American Jewish community.

For some Jews, the fact of membership in a Jewish organization is a manifest of membership in the Jewish community; for others, at least occasional contributions to the United Jewish Appeal. Will Maslow, in *The Structure and Functioning of the American Jewish Community*, is of the opinion that "as long as they consider themselves Jews, no matter what their affiliation (if any), they are part of that amorphous force known as the American Jewish community."

Within the framework of the American Jewish community, there is the widest possible diversity of thought on every conceivable subject—religious, political, educational, cultural. The common denominator lies in the fact that the people who hold these diverse and often antagonistic philosophies identify themselves as Jews. Many of them are members of organizations or institutions created to further the religious, cultural, educational, and other philosophies to which they are committed. To the same extent that self-declaration as a Jew (by anyone who, according to Jewish religious law, has the right to be so considered) is voluntary, so the end result—being considered a member of the Jewish community—is simply incidental to that self-indicated status.

Who speaks for the American Jewish community? More precisely, who speaks with its proven or articulated consent? Despite a conviction held by a great many non-Jews that such is the solidarity of Jews that whoever speaks as a Jew speaks for all, the truth is otherwise. There is no Great Assembly, no Sanhedrin, no Steering Committee for American Jewry that, after due deliberation, speaks with the united voice of the American Jew. That does not mean to say that organizations and single individuals or groups of individuals do not reflect very widely held Jewish concerns. It simply means that there is no single national Jewish organization to which has been given the authority to speak on all matters on behalf of the American Jewish community; there exists no instrument through which such authority can be given. The nearest American Jewry has come to a central authority is the Conference of Presidents of Major Jewish Organizations, which is a sort of unofficial spokesman for the national community.

How does a Jewish community "happen"? As has been stated, from earliest times, Jewish institutions and organizations have come into being in response to felt need. The first Jewish settlers in a community might very well organize to purchase a bit of land for a cemetery and only thereafter build a synagogue. It is understandable. One can worship anywhere—in a residence or a hall—but the dead must be laid to rest in a Jewish cemetery, in properly hallowed ground.

As their numbers increase, there is need for the Jewish education of the children, for looking after families or individuals who are in distress, for helping the transient on his way, and above all, for creating some sort of organization through which funds are to be raised for these and other needs.

In due time, the scattered Jewish communities, small and large alike, created patterns of organization, some of them purely local, but most of them bound into a network with national headquarters.

So that the reader of this guide can more easily find his way through the machinery of Jewish activity—local, national, and overseas—we will create a theoretical community whose size and needs make desirable, possible, and necessary an organizational pattern which would be similar to that to be found in a modest-sized American Jewish community.

Central to all activities in the theoretical community is what we will designate as the "Jewish Community Council." It could as readily be called the Jewish Federation and Council, or simply the Federation. By and large, names reflect the original functions for which the organization was created. Such central bodies had their historical antecedents in the European countries from which American Jews had come since the middle of the nineteenth century, and of course Jewry as a whole had the millennia-long tradition of mutual assistance. It was left to the American experience to elaborate the tradition into forms of association and activity that reflected conditions in this country.

Our hypothetical Jewish Community Council is made up of a number of component parts, principal among which are those that are concerned with social welfare programs, fund-raising, community relations and education, and possibly cultural needs. The conduct of its business rests in the hands of men and women who by reason of status in religious, educational, cultural, and other organizations, or of generosity with respect to Jewish causes, have evidenced qualities of leadership. An important, perhaps *the* most important, function of the council is to raise funds and to allocate them according to the relative needs of local, national, and overseas Jewish organizations.

Many Christian denominations have synods, district organizations, and national bodies whose funds are available for assistance to local churches, missions, church-related colleges, and the like. Jewish congregations do not have a comparable structure. Local congregations are not funded by the community council—nor, for that matter, by any other body; they maintain themselves through annual pledges and supplementary fund-raising projects. There are no collections at Jewish worship services; pledges are paid into the congregational treasury at agreed-upon intervals.

The tradition of Jewish education described in an earlier chapter persists into modern times. In fact, together with synagogue worship, Jewish education is one of the most deeply rooted traditions of Jewish life. The extent of community support of Jewish education through the council may depend upon factors related to the number and influence of individuals calling for such support, the availability of funds, and so forth.

Jewish education usually takes the form of "religious schools" or "Sunday schools" conducted for the most part about two hours on Sunday morning, in the facilities of the various congregations. In addition, congregations may also provide weekday classes, usually for the teaching of Hebrew. All such congregational education units are commonly funded by the congregation itself.

The community as a whole may be called on for financial assistance in the case of so-called day schools, which correspond to Christian parochial schools, in which religious education is included as part of the general curriculum. Such communal aid may be requested when tuition and general contributions are insufficient to meet the budgetary needs of the school.

Communal support of Jewish education may extend to seminaries and other schools of higher learning, whose purpose is to train men—and now women—for rabbinical and academic positions.

There are no "church-related" colleges in American Jewish life, as they exist in the Christian denominational structure. Any institution of higher learning that feels it has good reason to do so may call upon the organized American Jewish communities for financial assistance. It is the task of our Jewish Community Council to evaluate the appeal and to make such determinations it feels to be just.

Our council has a Committee on Community Relations, whose executive head is usually a professional in this area of Jewish concern and who, while empowered by the "advise and consent" role of his committee or board to act with local autonomy, may also seek the guidance of the National Jewish Community Relations Advisory Council, which represents all other local community relations programs and is organized for common consultation and coordination where and when necessary. Not all Jewish communities have organized community relations programs, just as, for that matter, not all have community councils or social welfare federations. They simply function through ad hoc committees called into being as need arises. As far as community relations programs are concerned, they can have the qualities of either defense or outreach. On the one hand, defense may relate to activities designed to counteract anti-Semitic defamation, while on the other, it may be spelled out in terms of activities whose goal it is to help create the social stability that is based on equality of opportunity for all. Programs of this sort are not confined to the Jewish community; there are many Christian congregations that have community relations committees. At the local level, therefore, the Jewish community often finds allies in local churches who are prepared to make common cause in the effort to achieve social justice.

In the same manner, national organizations, whether Jewish or Christian, white or black, have on occasion found it both possible and desirable to cooperate in challenging undesirable social conditions. The principal instrument for social change, it would seem, is in the field of legislation. It has been said that goodwill cannot be legislated, but legislation can keep prejudice from being translated into discrimination.

The principal Jewish organizations at work in the field of community relations are the American Jewish Congress, the American Jewish Committee, and the Anti-Defamation League of the B'nai B'rith. Differences in philosophies of action coupled with the natural tendency of individuals to develop procedures conforming to those philosophies brought about the organization of three rather than one all-embracing organization. It must be made clear, however, that both the American Jewish Congress and the American Jewish Committee have stated objectives and purposes that are broader than the advancement of civil rights alone. This is also true of the B'nai B'rith, parent organization of the Anti-Defamation League.

The "outreach" aspect of the work of community relations includes all activities whose purpose is to create better understanding of Judaism and the Jewish people. Rabbis and laymen alike are often invited to speak to church groups on subjects about which such groups may feel they need to be better informed. This sort of presentation/dialogue is not confined to church groups, of course; interest in knowing more about aspects of the Jewish faith has for a long time been evidenced by public and private school classes, civic clubs, and college classes. All in all, the lines of communication between the Jew and his neighbor have become increasingly open, and while the fact of Jewish "otherness" has not disappeared—since it cannot—such communication has tended to wash out of "otherness" still-clinging elements of hostility. The very fact that the initiatives for discussions, lectures, and seminars have so often been taken by non-Jewish groups is a heartening demonstration that old barriers are crumbling away.

If the guide has given more attention to the problems of group relations than to other areas of community activity, it is because they are a particularly sensitive complex of concerns.

iii

There is a Hebrew saying: "All Jews are dependent upon each other." The wording can also be translated: "All Jews are responsible for each other." This principle guides the efforts of what is known to the Jewish community as the United Jewish Appeal. The UJA has a rough correspondence to periodic Christian church appeals for missions and food and clothing distribution on an international scale, and various other efforts to alleviate the distress brought about by natural and man-made disasters. The United Jewish Appeal is, in effect, an umbrella organization whose funds are allocated to participating agencies occupied with welfare, medical care, and settlement and rehabilitation programs in various countries.

Like a local United Fund, the fund-raising is on an annual basis. If published figures show a very high level of contribution to the appeal, the reasons are not hard to find; the traditional generosity of the Jewish community, the once-a-year nature of the funding effort, the world-wide needs, and finally, the simple fact that Jews can look to no source of help other than themselves.

If, by now, the reader has the impression that the individual Jew is in one way or another an integral part of the local, national, and overseas components that make up Jewish communities, wherever they may be, the impression is well founded. Men and women in the armed services, students on college campuses, prisoners in jail and penitentiary, homeless transients, the helpless aging, individuals in need of vocational retraining, migrants in search of a new home—all need the kind of services that knowing and caring can provide. The Jewish student foundations (Hillel), chaplaincies, and homes for the aged are all expressions of the Jewish community in action.

Of all such felt needs, those that concern the State of Israel brought into existence, among others, the women's Zionist organization known as Hadassah. With over 350,000 members in communities scattered across the United States, Hadassah, organized in 1912 and from the beginning dedicated to providing medical services in what was then Palestine, has been a powerful and enormously effective agency for even more extensive services. Out of its response to obvious needs a whole network of hospitals, clinics, and medical training facilities was established in Israel. In addition, in 1935 Hadassah entered into a child rescue program to save young people from the Nazi danger, a concern that has since become a full-scale youth program in Israel.

The Jewish community is obviously a busy "enterprise," which, when in full realization of potential activity, reflects and fulfills the ancient saying of Rabbi Hillel: "Do not separate yourself from the community." Hillel could not have foreseen the contemporary Jewish need to meet the many claims made upon its human and material resources, but his additional saying stands as applicable: "If I am not for myself, who will be for me? But if I am for myself alone, what am I?—And if not now, when?"

iv

A closing reflection: we have ranged over a broad expanse of American Jewish community life, in its many aspects and statements, although touching down only here and there. The full range of institutional and organizational life is, even for the average Jew, quite astonishing. The multiplicity of the needs is in turn multiplied by the diversity of points of view on how to meet those needs.

The Jewish community is not unique in the effort to create such institutions and organizations; all American religious groupings are involved in comparable efforts. Their objective is to maintain the cohesiveness of their respective faiths or denominations and at the same time to fulfill religious teachings by attending to the requirements of the disadvantaged and victimized.

The difference may probably be said to lie in this: that the activities of the Jewish community, while also reflecting spiritual/social values inherent in Judaism, are the result of historic experience whose threat to both faith and folk intensified the will to survive, and survival calls for mechanisms of survival, as was noted earlier. Social welfare and social action programs alike are part of that mechanism. There is no Jewish organization or institution, local, national, or overseas, whether small or large, that is not an expression of that mechanism.

"Community" in any and all of its ramifications is rarely visible. It was for that reason that it was considered helpful to lead the reader through the door that opens into this very large room of Jewish folk life.

12
ZIONISM AND ISRAEL

From the beginning, "the land" had a very special mystique for the Jewish people. All the roads of Jewish history pointed toward it. God said to Abram, "I will give this land to your offspring" (Gen. 12:7); to Jacob He had promised, "the ground on which you are lying, I will give to you and to your offspring. . . . I will protect you until I have done what I promised you" (Gen. 28:12, 15). The end of the road on the long trek from Egypt, under Moses' leadership, was that Promised Land. There the tribes were to settle down; there too, David was to make Jerusalem his capital, and Solomon to build God's house, the great Temple.

Over the centuries, the very earth became sanctified by the footsteps of the men whose preaching and teaching called errant generations to order—God's order: the prophets whose clarification of the role of God in the life of man has not yet ceased reverberating:

> It shall ultimately come to pass, that the mountain of the Lord's house will be established as the very peak of the mountains, aloft the hills. And all nations will come streaming to it; many people shall come and

say, "Come! let us ascend to God's mount, to the house of the God of Jacob. He will teach us His ways and we will walk in His paths." For out of Zion shall go forth Torah, and the word of the Lord from Jerusalem. He will judge between nations, arbitrate between many peoples. They shall beat their swords into ploughshares, their spears into pruning hooks; nation shall not lift up sword against nation, nor shall they ever again study warring. O House of Jacob, come, let us walk in God's light! (Isa. 2:2–5).

The very genius of the prophetic message finds statement here: a messianic vision of mankind unified under God, at peace, turning from destruction and imposed death. At the heart of the message is one line: "For out of Zion shall go forth Torah." At the crossroads of the land is Jerusalem; atop Mt. Zion, the Temple. Zion thus became the symbol for Jerusalem, the locale for God's revelation to man, his teaching.

And all—mount, temple, city, messianic vision—gave sanctity to the whole land. The people had for so long associated self, land, and God as interfabricated, the pattern set by promise and historic fulfillment, that exile from the land was almost beyond understanding.

By the rivers of Babylon . . . we wept when we remembered Zion.
How shall we sing the Lord's song on alien soil?
If I forget you, O Jerusalem,
May my right hand forget its skill.
May my tongue cleave to the roof of my mouth
If I do not keep you always in mind;
If I do not elevate Jerusalem
Above my highest joy (Ps. 137:1, 4–6).

They would return from that exile in Babylon and under the leadership of Ezra and Nehemiah begin the reconstruction of life on the land. From that generation on, the kinship of people to land was even more firmly set, even though by those closing days great Jewish settlements had grown in both Babylonia and Egypt.

It would never matter where the migrants settled, or for what reason; it was to Jerusalem that they turned as the historic focus of Jewish identity. For long centuries to come, they would feel themselves to be strangers in strange lands, and, indeed, until they were granted citizenship in the lands of their residence, they were accounted strangers. Even when under Islamic rule the Jews of Spain enjoyed what has come to be known as their Golden Age, the poet Yehudah Halevi would write of Jerusalem, "The air of your land is the very life of our soul."

The assuring message of the prophet who lived to experience the Babylonian exile found its fulfillment fifty years later (c. 536 B.C.E.) when the Persian ruler, Cyrus, authorized and encouraged return and reconstruction. The Prophet Jeremiah had said, "Keep your voice from weeping, and your eyes from tears; for your work shall be rewarded, says the Lord, and they shall come back from the land of the enemy. There is hope for your future, says the Lord, and your children shall come back to their own country" (Jer. 31:15–17).

His words, together with the many others that spelled out promise, hope, and assurance, were a source of encouragement to the people in final exile when, in 135 C.E., the uprising led by Bar Kohba ended in bloody failure. As noted earlier, Jerusalem's very name was changed to Aelia Capitolina, and entry therein was barred to Jews by the Roman authority. It was, until modern times, the last effort to reconstitute an autonomous Jewish state.

ii

For almost two millennia, Jews wandered the face of the earth, settling here and there for brief or for long periods of time, depending on the capricious fortunes spun by both church and civil rulers. The circumstances of life in Christian Europe ranged from extortionate taxation to forced baptism, from humiliating badges and "Jew hats" to pillage and arson, from enforced residence in ghettoes to massacre and exile. At no time was the Jew allowed to forget that he was "other," subject to a demeaning existence because of his blind stubbornness in refusing to accept Jesus as the Christ, and—worse—because of the charge of deicide, killers of God's Son.

The pressures and abnormalities of Jewish existence gave rise to fantasies of hope centered around the coming of messianic leadership, under whose banner the people would be restored to the ancient land. Men did in fact appear now and then who proclaimed themselves to be the awaited Messiah, but the end of it all was disillusionment and despair. Outstanding among the claimants was Shabbetai Z'vi, who gained a multitude of followers whose high expectations were brought to a bitter conclusion by Z'vi's conversion, in 1666, to Mohammedanism. It was a betrayal of stunning dimension.

The hope for return to the land never died; it was kept alive day after day in the prayers of the siddur. In his *Jewish Worship*, Abraham Millgram describes such prayer as a "holding action, as it were." There can be no mistake about the meaning of the words of this prayer:

> Sound the great horn of our freedom; raise the ensign
> to gather our exiles and gather us from the four cor-

ners of the earth. Blessed art thou, O Lord, who gath-
erest the dispersed of thy people Israel.

Speedily cause the offspring of David, thy servant, to
flourish, and lift up his glory by thy divine help, because we wait for thy salvation all the day. . . .

And return in mercy to Jerusalem, Thy city, and
dwell therein as Thou has spoken; rebuild it soon in
our days as an everlasting building, and speedily set
up therein the throne of David. Blessed art Thou, O
Lord, who rebuildest Jerusalem.

After every meal these words were included in the
grace: "Let us O Lord, our God, behold the consolation of
Zion, thy city, and the rebuilding of Jerusalem, thy holy
city, for Thou art the Lord of salvation and consolation."
Even in the marriage service there were heard the words of
expectation and hope: "Soon may there be heard in the
cities of Judah, and in the streets of Jerusalem, the voice of
joy and gladness. . . ."

The most clearly enunciated words of hope were written
into the service for the Passover seder. As culmination to
the story of the redemption of Egypt, and acutely aware of
their status as nonpersons in newer Egypts, the participants in the ancient ritual of salvation proclaimed,
"LeShanah HaBaah B'yrushalayim!"—Next year in
Jerusalem!

That is what "Zionism" was all about. It was the dream
of return to the ancient land. The use of words like
redemption and *salvation* were not theological as in the
Christian understanding of such words; nor did the "setting up of the throne of David" have messianic implications as in Christianity when in the New Testament Jesus'

genealogy was traced back to David (Matt. 1:6–14). This Jewish use of *redemption* and *salvation* applied quite simply to relief, through God's intervention, from the painful abnormalities of Jewish folk existence. It was the hope for a life within which the Jew would not be subject to the capricious and hostile decisions of men and mobs influenced by prejudice, hate, or greed. It was the old prophetic vision of a place and time where and when each man would sit without fear, secure, under his vine and under his fig tree.

That does not mean to imply that there were no Jews resident in the land. Actually, there never was a time when the ancient land was without a Jewish population. In *The Jews in Their Land*, edited by David Ben-Gurion, the history of the Jewish settlement is carefully traced. It is an interesting story and can be read with profit.

But the centuries-long, scattered settlement under successive rulers is not the same as restoration of Jewish autonomy as it was in Bible times. The vision of that restoration was vague; all it really did was to keep alive the viability of the land as the ultimate answer to the deeply felt the needs of the people. How could it be otherwise? For this was the land to which God, in covenant with the people, had led them. This was the land where the Torah had its setting. This was the land where the genius of the Jewish people came to full flower. The Jews of the Diaspora could not envision their condition as being anything but temporary, even though "temporary" was stretched out over the centuries.

The Jew did not speak of a Diaspora or dispersion; he spoke of *galut*, exile. The sense of being in exile would possibly not have been sustained had the Jew been fully received as an equal, a man among men, wherever he found place to lay his head. And when, finally, in Western

Europe, restrictive legislation came to an end and the Jew was accorded full citizenship status free of former disabilities, Reform Judaism did in fact reinterpret the dispersion from being a condition of exile to one fulfilling the "Mission of Israel." For the implication of exile was that the Jew was in temporary residence everywhere, that he was simply marking time until the day of return to the land. On the other hand, the concept of mission held that the dispersion was part of God's plan to give opportunity to his people to become a "light unto the nations . . . ," an everlasting vocation.

It was because of this difference of theological interpretation as to the meaning of the dispersion that Reform Judaism rejected Zionism as a tenet of its basic doctrinal beliefs until over a century after its founding.

iii

The dream of return even when coupled with actual sporadic settlement of individuals is not the same as a movement impelled by the dream but, above all, organized for structured life. There had to be a bridge from the ages-old dream of redemptive messianism to the modern concept of nationalism. What would be the instrumentality for return—a messianic individual who was clearly God's agent, or a movement shaped by men and their visions of the how, the why, and the when?

Arthur Hertzberg, in his *Introduction to the Zionist Idea*, writes,

From the Jewish perspective messianism and not nationalism, is the primary element in Zionism. The very name of the movement evoked the dream of an end of days, of an ultimate release from exile and a coming to rest in the land of Jewry's heroic age. . . . Writers . . . have characterized the modern movement as "secular messianism," to indicate at once what is classical in Zionism—its eschatological purpose; and what is modern—the necessarily contemporary tools of political effort, colonization, and the definition of Jewry as a nation, thereby laying claim to the inalienable right to self-determination.

The reader, aware of the existence of the State of Israel, may wonder why it is felt to be necessary to trace the beginnings of modern Zionism.

The answer is that Zionism, with its culmination in the establishment of the State of Israel, touched the raw nerve of the Jewish historic experience. There was almost feverish excitement in the thought that after two thousand years there might once more be established an autonomous Jewish state on the ancient land. No matter what political factors were involved, there were messianic overtones. The philosophers and visionaries of modern Zionism wrote and spoke of their hopes for the people reborn; their dreams embraced exalted visions of the reconstruction of individual and people alike. An early song proclaimed, "Come let us go to the Land, to build it and to be rebuilt by it." Zionism is the very pulse of the Jewish heart; it is far less a question of Israel as a modern state than it is of Israel as the symbol of Jewish survival and continuity. In a world reverberating with assaults against "political Zionism," as though it were something diabolic, it is imperative—morally imperative—that the truth be clearly seen. For "political Zionism" was simply the theory of Jewish statehood as a political entity, rather than as a vaguely structured spiritual center for the Jews of the Diaspora, or a nebulous cultural center that would somehow transmit to that Diaspora the products of Jewish cultural life, however such products were envisioned.

iv

What gave the strongest impetus to modern Zionism was an event that occurred in the year 1894. Capt. Alfred Dreyfus, a Jew and general staff officer in the French army, was charged with treason and espionage for having passed military secrets to the Germans. Convicted by a military court, he was publicly degraded and sentenced to life imprisonment on Devil's Island. In time it became evident that Captain Dreyfus had been falsely accused, and that the documents used against him had been forged. Even at that, it was five years before he was fully exonerated. The Dreyfus Affair, as it came to be called, brought into play all the seemingly stilled anti-Semitism resident in large segments of the French population. The entire country was split into hostile sides.

Theodor Herzl, playwright, essayist, and journalist, who was at this time correspondent for a Viennese daily newspaper, had earlier become interested in the phenomenon of anti-Semitism in France. With the trial of Captain Dreyfus, which he covered, and the subsequent outbursts of virulent anti-Semitism, he came to the conclusion that if such events could occur in Europe's most highly civilized country, the first to legally emancipate the Jews, then there was no hope for the Jews of Europe save to create their own state elsewhere. Out of his reflections on this problem, there emerged in 1896 a small book entitled *The*

Jewish State, which became the guidebook of the seedling political Zionist movement. Accepted by many save strongly assimilationist Jews and those Orthodox Jews who looked for messianic solutions, *The Jewish State* rallied all Jewish leaders who were ready for the political action it called for and who constituted the membership of the first Zionist Congress, which assembled in Basel, Switzerland, in 1897.

The rest is modern Jewish history. The years between 1897 and the critical year 1917 were years of strenuous effort to obtain the backing of national regimes, of czar and kaiser and sultan. They were also years of ongoing migration to Palestine by small groups of Jews, pressed by the violence of czarist Russia, by disillusionment with the superficial effects of the Emancipation, and stimulated by the exciting possibility of folk renewal in the ancient land. Small colonies were established and experiments in collective settlement entered into.

On November 2, 1917, the movement toward autonomy as a Jewish state was given the official recognition of a world power, Great Britain. The so-called Balfour Declaration is of historic importance in the life of the Jewish people, and therefore merits being presented here in its entirety:

> Dear Lord Rothschild,
> I have much pleasure in conveying to you, on behalf of his Majesty's Government, the following declaration of sympathy with Jewish Zionist aspirations which has been submitted to, and approved by, the Cabinet.
> "His Majesty's Government views with favour the establishment in Palestine of a national home for the Jewish people, and will use their best

endeavours to facilitate the achievement of this object, it being clearly understood that nothing shall be done which may prejudice the civil and religious rights of existing non-Jewish communities in Palestine, or the rights and political status enjoyed by Jews in any other country."

I would be grateful if you would bring this declaration to the knowledge of the Zionist Federation.

The letter was signed by Arthur James Balfour, then British foreign secretary.

It was the first time since the loss of Jewish independence in 70 C.E. that a power of any standing, let alone one of Great Britain's magnitude, had recognized the Jews as a people entitled to a homeland. The declaration was ultimately incorporated in the mandate of the League of Nations, which, thirty years after the promulgation of the declaration, voted for the creation of a Jewish state in Palestine.

The story of Zionism and Israel would be incomplete without comments on two major elements: the Holocaust and the "Arab problem."

Stated coldly and objectively—to the extent that a Jew can be either cold or objective when discussing the Holocaust—the Nazi regime between the years 1941 and 1945 brought about the destruction of six million Jews—men, women, and children alike—through various means, chief among which were the gas ovens of the concentration camps. Before the Holocaust there was a world Jewish population of eighteen million. The loss of a third of world Jewry, and under such circumstances, had a profoundly traumatic effect on the Jewish people, particularly since it was clear that the world powers at war with Germany were not willing to take the necessary steps to save the doomed Jews of Europe.

The horror of those years of the death camps can scarcely be encompassed by the human mind. The ultimate in the dehumanization of the victims was achieved in the rendering of what fat was left on emaciated bodies to make soap, the flaying of bodies to make lampshades of the skin, medical experiments upon living bodies. Jews especially, but also other categories of "undesirables," became not just nonpersons but nonhuman; their treatment put them into the category of human trash.

The nightmare phenomena of those years took decades to confront and put into perspective. These words of Arthur A. Cohen give some inkling of the meaning of the Holocaust. Referring to past writing about tragic confrontations he writes.

> . . . the evil about us [was] visible and identifiable, and the thrust of virtue [remained] potent and vivifying. The holocaust has demolished that universe. . . . Not a single question that animated the moral universe of their precursors . . . remains visible. Death and dying are not interesting . . . the separation of man and animals meaningless; the violation of children pedestrian. Name any value, anything human beings treasure as precious and inalienable, and the literature of atrocity has exhibited that far from being inviolate, it was violated as a matter of course.

The widening destruction of the Jewish people under the demonic assaults of the Nazis made clear that the entire Jewish civilization of both Western and Eastern Europe would be demolished to rubble. Under the circumstances, the existence of a Jewish collective presence in Palestine as a place of refuge for all who could be saved from the Holocaust appeared to be in a literal sense providential. The physical bodies of six million Jews had been gunned down into mass graves or had gone up in the smoke of the death camps, but, phoenixlike, nascent Israel seemed to have been born for this evil day. Heroic efforts were made to bring in—even though illegally, under the strictures of the British Mandatory Administration—the Jewish escapees from the furnaces of Nazism.

One cannot understand the Israelis without knowing something about the Holocaust. By the time the State of Israel came into existence as such, the memory and meaning of the Holocaust was deeply encapsulated in the Israeli mind. If a historic lesson emerged, it was probably this: that the Jewish people must look to themselves for their salvation. It was a bitter lesson.

v

In July 1969 Abba Eban, then foreign minister of the State of Israel, said: "The only course is to promote an intimate link with the Palestinian Arabs without now closing the probability that they have a future separate from ours. Much can be done in the provision of services, livelihood, investment, economic stimulation, commerce and ordinary plain human encounter. But this is no substitute for the large vision of peace with the whole Arab world." In the year in which this is being written, there is clearly no peace with the Arab world. To the contrary, there have been bloody encounters with terrorists based in Arab countries, economic boycotts, worldwide diplomatic moves to isolate Israel, and defamation from the lectern of the United Nations.

The story of Jewish faith and folk cannot be written without telling the story of Zionism and Israel, but it in turn cannot be told without some understanding of the Arab problem.

The Arabs of Palestine had, over the centuries, many rulers, the most recent of which, at the time of the Balfour Declaration, had been the Ottoman Empire. Because the Ottoman sultan allied himself with Germany in World War I, the empire went down to defeat when Germany was defeated, and northern and southern Palestine were mandated to France and Great Britain, respectively, by the League of Nations. Palestine was therefore under the British mandate from 1922 to British withdrawal upon relinquishing the mandate in 1948.

While still under Ottoman rule, the Arabs of Palestine nurtured an embryonic national movement, which oscillated between hostility to, and acceptance of, the Zionist presence in the land. There never was a "Jewish invasion" of Palestine; all land in those premandate years had been bought and paid for. It was the Arab landowners themselves who saw opportunity for substantial profit in these transactions; dislocation of the tenants was sometimes a by-product of the sale of land to the incoming settlers. But the dislocations were few, for the lands that became Jewish holdings were marsh or rocky. The record of early Jewish settlements is a record of malaria, backbreaking toil, and pioneering effort to redeem the soil.

Underlying the sporadic conflict between Arabs and Jews, which saw its most ferocious statement in the Arab massacres of 1929, was the head-on collision of two nationalisms. For Zionism, although rooted in ages-old alienation from ancient Israel, was catapulted into its modern political form amid the developing nationalisms of the nineteenth and twentieth centuries. Zionism was thus a sort of religio-nationalism, a folk-nationalism.

When Great Britain received the mandate from the League of Nations in 1922, there was no Palestinian state. The name "Palestine" became an accepted and official term when, in the terms of the mandate, the area was designated "Mandated Palestine." At that time, Palestine included territory that is now the State of Jordan. To the Jews, Palestine was known only as *Eretz Yisrael*, the Land of Israel, or, more simply, *HaAretz*, The Land.

It was to resolve the problem of meeting the needs of both populations that on November 21, 1947, the United Nations, which in 1945 had become the successor organization to the League of Nations, approved a partition plan that created both a Jewish state and an Arab state in western Palestine, with an international sector in Jerusalem. Jewish institutions accepted the resolution, even though the state was a distorted, gerrymandered fragment of what was originally hoped for.

However, the Arabs rejected the resolution and initiated a war with the newborn Jewish state, with the objective of destroying it in its infancy and then taking over the entire mandatory territory. The same objective brought about the wars of 1967 and 1973, but the results were far from what the Arabs had hoped for. Important Arab territories had to be yielded to the Israelis, and large numbers of Arabs came under Israeli military control in what were known as the Administered Territories. From then on the Arab world sought to obtain through terrorism and world economic pressures what it could not win on the battlefield.

At the heart of the (thus far) unresolved conflict was the issue of Palestinian rights. An important element in the

Arab demand for the realization of those rights was the question of the so-called Palestinian refugees. "So-called" because their identity, their numbers, and their status as refugees are the subject of controversy. The records show that in 1947 between 500,000 and 600,000 Arabs left Israel and crossed into Arab territories. Not all Arabs fled; those who remained became citizens of Israel. Those who left Israel were housed in refugee camps in the countries of their new residence, and there they were allowed to remain by the host countries, who denied them the right of assimilation and integration into a normal productive life. They became the wards of the United Nations Relief Agency.

The charge has been made over the years that these "refugees" were thrust out by Israel. The record of those early days shows beyond any reasonable doubt that Arab leaders stimulated the mass flight, expecting a quick victory over the State of Israel followed by the triumphant return of the fleeing Arabs.

To this day these people have been the unfortunate victims of Arab miscalculation coupled with indifference to the misery of their fellows. Is there the possibility that they will indeed share with their fellow Arabs in the Israeli-administered territories a still-to-be-created Palestinian state?

The currents of history move fast, and man never twice puts his hand in the same waters. At the time these words were written, the State of Israel had again officially expressed its readiness to enter into negotiations with any Arab state that, with respect to the Palestinian problem, recognized Israel's right to national existence within secure borders.

vi

Whatever will have happened in the arena of mideastern and world diplomacy by the time these pages reach the public eye, the purpose of this book will not have been achieved if this basic fact is not reiterated: that, for the Jew, Israel is the symbol of Jewish existence everywhere. At the outset of this chapter on Zionism and Israel, it was stated: "From the beginning, 'The Land' had a very special mystique for the Jewish people." By our own day, mystique had given way to urgent need for many, and psychological fulfillment for most, just because it symbolized deeply felt needs of the individual Jew and of the Jewish people as a whole.

What was, and probably always will be, at issue is the right to be, to exist, and to have the right to existence acknowledged and respected. That is why the worldwide Jewish interest in the fate and fortunes of the State of Israel is so strong. In those national experiences, the Jew sees—and feels—a mirroring of his own historic experience as a people, and a projection of his future.

13
SOME BYPATHS

*Hebrew and Yiddish—the Languages of
Faith and Folk*

i

Until modern times, Hebrew had been regarded solely as
the sacred tongue of the Jewish faith. It did not lose that
characteristic but gained an additional identity as a
spoken secular language.

It was the language in which God revealed himself to the
people, the speech of the people in their worship. Scriptures and liturgy alike are written in the ancient tongue. So
also are various postbiblical literatures extending into
modern times: commentaries, homiletical writing, essays
on religious subjects.

Every Jewish child was expected to be sufficiently well
educated in the reading and comprehension of Hebrew to
be, at the very least, at home in the ancient prayers; at
best, it was hoped that he would achieve distinction as a
scholar of the biblical texts and commentaries, as well as
become an expert—perhaps even outstanding—on the

Talmud and its commentaries. Literacy was never merely for its own sake: To know the word, so to speak, was to know the path to God. Not to be versed in Hebrew was to be almost illiterate in a spiritual sense.

Without doubt, there never was a time when Jews were not capable of writing in Hebrew, and when necessary, of communicating with each other in that language. But such writing and communication were largely reserved for subject matter that merited its utilization, and thus those who used it were more the scholarly and creative few than the mass of the people. We know that there were periods of time when the people lost contact with Hebrew; when the Torah was read in public, translation into the vernacular had to accompany the reading.

The capability of Hebrew as a creative language was fully evidenced during the so-called Golden Age of Jewish history when from about the middle of the tenth century to the end of the fifteenth the Jews of Spain were under Islamic rule. That period saw the birth of a whole literature that included poetic, philosophical and grammatical works. But although some of the poetry was secular in content, the ancient tongue still carried the flavor of an older day. It was far from being a folk language, and certainly no effort was made to have it so. The time was far from ready for those great changes of folk life and self-understanding, which would turn to the deliberate cultivation of Hebrew as an element in the building of a new Jewish identity.

We have entered into the discussion of Hebrew—as of Yiddish—because the language through which a people expresses itself, and the relative importance given to the language, tells us a great deal about that people. Our purpose has been to present the reader with a comprehensive understanding of the Jewish faith and folk. That understanding would be incomplete if there were missing an account of how the language of faith became the language of more secular statement.

When and why did it happen? What has been its effect upon Jewish life?

The great winds of change that blew over Europe had their greatest velocity and impact during the eighteenth century, which witnessed the French revolution, the Age of Enlightenment, and the Industrial Revolution. The economic, political, and intellectual changes that came to maturity during this era had deep and lasting effect on Jewish life. The Jew was at last enabled to move out of his shadowed existence in the ghetto into the brighter light of the new day. With emancipation, there came the intel ctuals' call for the full exploration of this bright new world.

In Eastern Europe, particularly in Russia, Poland, and Romania, which remained relatively untouched by the new age, there was strong resistance to the implications of emancipation. Fearing a breakdown in the coherence of Jewish life, orthodoxy set itself against alterations that might take away from that life the values that had held it together, and might even lead to the ultimate dissolution of historic Judaism.

On the other hand, proponents of the new Jewish enlightenment (*Haskalah*) were strongly committed to the thought that it was time for the Jewish people to break the confines of all limitations that deprived it of the opportunity to be fulfilled in the largest possible way.

Out of the Haskalah movement there came a generation of intellectuals, essayists, poets, novelists, dramatists, and philosophers, as well as of writers in all fields of contemporary knowledge, who thus opened wide the windows to show the larger vistas of spiritual and intellectual potential. The language of the Haskalah was Hebrew. Based upon the ancient vocabularies of the entire range of biblical and postbiblical writing, including medieval literature of a nonreligious character, the language was molded and shaped to express more contemporary thoughts. What had occurred from the late eighteenth through the nineteenth centuries was a great spiritual revival, which turned to Hebrew as the chosen instrument of its expression.

Thus the groundwork was laid for the first settlements in Palestine, whose pioneers had from their childhood looked upon Hebrew as the mother tongue of the national renaissance and renascence.

The influence of the Hebrew revival has been very pervasive. Thanks in part to the long-standing role of Hebrew as the sacred language, and in part due to the extraordinary impact of the establishment of the State of Israel, Hebrew is studied today not only in congregational Sunday and weekday schools but in adult-education courses as well. Here and there groups gather to make the language the vehicle of their common discourse. Journals are published to assist the student and the master alike; Jewish summer camps have introduced methods for the furtherance of understanding of the old/new tongue. Educational programs in Israel have attracted large numbers of American youth who have thus gained fluency in Hebrew.

The attraction of Hebrew can be easily understood. For a very long time, American Jews were urged to study in order to have at least a reading knowledge, in order to participate in worship services. The Zionist movement gave increasingly effective impulse to study Hebrew, for the sake of its status as the historic tongue of the people about to be reborn. Both reasons had their emotional underpinnings. The net result is that the study of Hebrew has had increasingly wide acceptance. For many, perhaps for most, Jews it has become a means for "hands across the sea" fellowship with the Jews of Israel.

But for all that, Hebrew cannot be called a folk language. It is the official language of Israel, and therefore the mother tongue of increasingly large numbers of Israelis born in the land. A folk language is one that is for everyone the currency of everyday usage, the vocabulary of people's thoughts and dreams, the vehicle of the novelist, poet, journalist, playwright. For the American Jew, that language is English.

And yet there still survive vestiges of a true Jewish folk language that, unlike Hebrew, was the common tongue of millions of Jews. The world that created it and nurtured it has been demolished, its teeming masses destroyed or scattered. Six million took their mother tongue into the mass graves and gas ovens of the Holocaust; but decades before that happened, others had taken it with them into newer lands as they fled from the violent oppression and economic hopelessness of their homelands. That language is Yiddish, and the reader is invited to consider some interesting aspects of that vital and colorful tongue.

ii

Although Yiddish is written in Hebrew characters, it is an entirely separate language. The origin of Yiddish has been traced by its major historian, Max Weinreich, to the Jewish communities that flourished along the Rhine and Moselle rivers in Germany about a thousand years ago. Jews came there from northern France and Italy. When, due to the massacres and pillaging of Crusaders on their way to the Holy Land, the German Jews fled to the safer territory of Poland, they took with them the makings of what was to develop as the Yiddish language. Basically, Yiddish is built upon a Germanic foundation, into which "foreign" words had already penetrated from the earlier Italian and French origins, and to which Slavic words and expressions were added. Of course, the daily contact with Hebrew made inevitable the introduction of both Hebrew words and Hebrew grammatical elements.

During the long history of Jewish life in Russia and Poland, Yiddish took on a special life and character, which intimately reflected every aspect of the Jewish soul. Like any true folk tongue, it was shaped to express every nuance of mind and spirit. With the barriers up between the Jew and his non-Jewish neighbor, there was never occasion for full usage of the national language. The circumstances of their group life threw them back upon their own internal mode of existence. There was considerable interaction between Jews and Christians in many spheres of daily life, but, as it has been said, Jews lived among non-Jews, but not with them.

When, in the late nineteenth and early twentieth centuries, great numbers of East European Jews emigrated from Poland and Russia to the United States, they brought Yiddish with them. While a determined effort was made to learn English as well, it was of course Yiddish that, as their *mama-loshen* (mother tongue), was the language of home and street, of shop and store, of stage, newspaper, and book.

Today Yiddish survives but is spoken or written far less extensively. Successive generations have become Americanized; for them, English is the mama-loshen. And yet, so colorful and precise was Yiddish in its penetrating understanding of how best to characterize the human experience that it has left its traces in the English language itself. For whatever reason it may have come about, the field of entertainment attracted large numbers of Jews, and it was probably they who made commonplace Yiddish words, to such an extent that non-Jews who know no other Yiddish vocabulary make apt use of such words as *kibitz, nebbish, shlemihl, mensh, goy, schlok,* and others. For those readers for whom some of these words may be unfamiliar, *The Joys of Yiddish* by Leo Rosten is heartily recommended. Since, however, that delightful "relaxed lexicon of Yiddish, Hebrew and Yinglish words often encountered in English" may not be at hand, some definitions of the above words are in order.

To kibitz is to butt in. It carries with it the overtone of making somebody's else's business your own. A shlemihl is luckless, butterfingered, and clumsy, someone who is socially inept—or generally so. Nebbish is closely related to shlemihl, but with an element of sadness and sympathy introduced. Rosten suggests that "a *nebech* [his preferred spelling] is more to be pitied than a *schlemiel* [variant spelling]. You feel sorry for a *nebech;* you *can* dislike a *schlemiel.*" A mensh is very much more than simply a man, a person (original German meaning); for the Jew to be a mensh is to be a person of respectability, dignity, and honor. A goy is a non-Jew, and schlok (or schlock) is any kind of cheap goods, shoddy materials.

In this generation, wherever there are large concentrations of Jews, even though its use has diminished considerably as a literary vehicle, Yiddish is still widely used—its use ranging from full folk tongue to a sort of nostalgic recall here and there, now and then, where the use of Yiddish words and expressions more aptly expresses the thought than would English. Historically, Yiddish must still be considered the language of the Jewish folk, but it is fighting a rearguard battle against the erosion of time and circumstances. Certainly this is true of Jews in the United States. Whether it is equally true of East European Jews who have settled in other lands is a question of interest, but we are concerned only with manifestations of Jewish faith and folk in the United States.

Hasidism

As a religious movement that began in the middle of the eighteenth century in that part of East Europe known as Poland-Lithuania, that grew to extraordinary dimensions only to wane in influence and importance, and that then transferred to the United States almost two hundred years after its origin to become a dynamic force in Jewish life, Hasidism merits description and comment. Thanks to occasional publicity in the mass media, sizable numbers of non-Jews who live outside the areas in which there are Hasidic communities have become more or less acquainted with at least some of the superficial aspects of the movement. What, then, is Hasidism?

The designation *Hasid* has the literal meaning of "pietist," an individual dedicated to a life of strict observance of ritual laws and to fulfilling the *mitzvot* (laws that, according to Jewish tradition, give regulatory guidance to living the good life, spiritually speaking). *Hasidim* is its plural form, and *Hasidism* designates the movement itself. But such a spare set of definitions gives no hint at all of the inner character of the movement; it does not explain the remarkable hold that it once had on the masses of East European Jews, nor does it explain its present strength.

Hasidism in its beginning had the character of a Jewish revival movement. It was, in a sense, waiting to be born. The early eighteenth century was a time of despair, misery, poverty, and disillusionment for most of the Jews of Eastern Europe. Preceding the rise of Hasidism, there had been the traumatic record of massacres and false Messiahs. The despair that both engendered found no helpful answer in the Jewish leadership of that era. The people were ready for a leadership and teaching that would restore to them their human dignity and justify the way of God with man.

The answer came in the person of one Israel ben Eliezer, known then and since as the Besht (acronym for *Baal SHem Tov*), Master of the Good Name—i.e., one who had the power effectively to invoke God's name for spiritual and curative purposes. Teaching through parables rather than sermonic exhortation, the Besht proclaimed that every man, no matter how lowly or ignorant, had access to God; that the religious status of the individual depended not on his scholarship but upon what we might today call his spiritual and workaday life-style. Indeed, he insisted, the very manner in which we carried out our daily lives could be an expression of our spiritual selves.

The road to spiritual fulfillment lay through joy; despair and depression belied man's faith in God and warped his ability to communicate with him. But even more was needed to lift man up: He must know how to pray; for prayer to ascend, the worshipper required *kavannah*, that strength of spiritual prompting that sped the prayer onward as though it were an arrow's flight impelled by the tautness of the string and guided by the inner vision. In addition, if the worshipper sought to find those forces within himself with which he could effect the ultimate goal of *dvekut*—God-closeness—he must turn up the pilot light of his desire into the intense fervor of *hitlahavut*—enflamement—as though his very being was on fire.

For the Hasid, God-closeness does not correspond to

the mystical concept of immersion of self in the great being of God. The ultimate objective is the purification of the soul so that the individual Jew can better carry out God's expectations in the bread-and-butter world of daily existence.

The teaching took hold, and there proliferated communities of Hasidism, whose pivotal center was the *tzaddik*, that very essence and personification of the Hasidic teachings, who became for his followers teacher, counselor, and leader, and who, in the aura of charisma that attached to him, was often deemed capable of miracles. His followers looked to him to help them resolve their problems, and drew from him something of the spiritual elevation with which they felt him to be endowed. Hasidism thus became a well-defined way of life, which moved beyond mere orthodoxy by providing a system of teachings that were constantly reinforced by the patterns of fellowship the movement created.

Movements of this sort are rarely able to maintain the initial dynamism of their beginnings. In time, Hasidism lost the mass base of its support, although there never was a time from then until today when Hasidic clusters did not exist, not only in Eastern Europe, but in Israel and in other countries as well.

"Other countries" includes our own. Hasidic groups came to the United States as part of the great waves of immigration between 1880 and 1925. But neither then nor now has the movement taken hold as in Eastern Europe; the historic events that gave rise to its origin in the eighteenth century no longer exist. In addition, the folk life of Eastern Europe that proved such fertile soil for Hasidism to flourish in has no parallel here, although our generation has been one of disillusionment and, Jewishly speaking, has been a period of great concern for the viability of traditional Jewish life. The influence of the general culture has proven destructive of many aspects of that life.

Some Hasidic groups have responded by withdrawing more firmly into the patterns of their life-style, clinging with even greater fervor to the outer signs of their tradition—the garb of older days in Eastern Europe, and of course the beard and *payot*, long earlocks, which are in fulfillment of the biblical ordinance not to cut the "corners of the beard" (Lev. 19:27; 21:5). However, an outstanding exception has been the so-called Lubavitcher Hasidic movement, which since about 1940 has entered upon a course of virtual "evangelization" of American Jewry and has been active in other countries as well. Funded by its worldwide following, the movement has founded schools and seminaries and a press for dissemination of its literature; retreats have been organized and emissaries have been sent out to the smaller Jewish communities to acquaint them with Hasidic doctrine and to urge return to traditional practices. Every effort is being made to persuade youth, especially in the large cities, that the Hasidic life-style is the answer to today's spiritual ills.

It is improbable that Hasidism will ever regain its original influence on the scale it once knew. But it has proven to be the answer for many young people, especially in the metropolitan areas, who find in its clear-cut regimen of life an anchorage in a world that has left them without moorings.

14
ON BEING A JEW

The foregoing pages describe the many facets of Jewish faith and folk, but they do not tell what it means to a Jew to be a Jew. It is far from a simple matter to lead a non-Jew into the inner heartland of the Jewish experience, all the more so since how the Jew reacts to events that touch his identity as Jew will vary from person to person. Quite aside from those elements that contribute to the psychological formulations of the individual character, there are the equally complex factors of religious training and response to it, general knowledge of, and reaction to, the events of Jewish history, and the person's life experience with Christian–Jewish relationships.

Taking all these factors into consideration, we can see why it is difficult to generalize about Jewish response to the Jewish experience.

Despite these difficulties, and because it would be helpful for the reader to have some understanding of what it means to be a Jew, this guide will undertake to describe a dual experience. The first is that of "the Jew in the world"; the second, "the world in the Jew."

In what follows, there is much that is personal to the

writer, but I believe that I speak for most of my fellow Jews.

The Jew in the World

We Jews have a sort of multiple existence: individually, we live in one place, one land, but we have deep emotional bonds with our fellow Jews everywhere. Wherever there are Jews, there is a felt kinship. What happens to Jews, as Jews, anywhere in the world, touches all of us. There may be differences between us—language, dress, custom, religious outlook, even color—but within the framework of the Jewish historical experience the differences are superficial, even irrelevant. What is important is that we see the Jewish experience anywhere as having meaning for us everywhere.

It is for that reason that we Jews, by and large, lead a somewhat uneasy life. That does not mean that there is an ever-present feeling of tension, and certainly not of danger. To the contrary, like every other average person, the Jew goes about his daily bread-and-butter tasks, preoccupied with those concerns that are part of everyone's workaday life—work, business, home, children, bills, taxes, and the like. But the special concerns of Jewish life penetrate into the more private individual domain. We Jews never really have a purely private domain alone, without regard to the needs of others. Our lives are interfabricated with those of all other Jews. The misfortunes of our people anywhere do not go unheeded. It is the realization that there are still such misfortunes that was in mind when it was said that by and large we lead a somewhat uneasy life.

Anti-Semitism is still deeply rooted in Western civilization, and for many of us there is the conviction that this moral disease will never be completely cured. It has many faces, some of them hatefully malevolent, others facile and polite. In the Soviet Union it has expressed itself in decades-long efforts to hack at the roots of Jewish religious and cultural life, as well as to impede every effort to emigrate to more favorable lands. In our own country, what we encounter is for the most part frustrating, irritating, and elusive rather than forthright and abrasive, ranging from myths about our wealth and power to vandalism in our cemeteries. They are minor, and we can live with these experiences.

What we do not know is the extent to which anti-Semitic feelings lie dormant, feelings that possible economic or political disaster might bring into the open, to our detriment and hurt. If it is contended that such concerns are paranoid fantasies, that there is no chance that "it can happen here," we can only reply that long centuries of being singled out as scapegoats, and thus natural victims, have made us singularly wary. Historic anti-Semitism is no longer religious, but its effect has been to create an image of us that lends itself to exploitation when human psychological needs require it. To be "other" is to be vulnerable.

What is it that we are looking for, we Jews? What do we ask of this frustrating world? Certainly not special treatment. We ask nothing more than to be accepted for what we are, and that "what we are" be seen free of the accretions of myths and legends. It is perhaps a utopian, an almost messianic expectation. But we Jews have a very strong messianic streak. However, our more mature and sophisticated understanding of the nature of modern society and its available tools for social reform has led us to the conclusion that to normalize our existence we must do two things: On the one hand, there is need for in-depth dialogue with Christian scholars and leaders, and on the other, there is need for the kind of efforts that will bring about justice through law. The former—dialogue—has as its goal the alteration of historic Christian theological positions that played a formative role in the creation and strengthening of myths about the Jew, attitudes that led to persecution and social disability. The latter—justice through law—has as its prime goal the undergirding of existing laws and the promulgation of new ones to make difficult, if not impossible, the translation of prejudice into discrimination.

Of course, we Jews know that this is a vast assignment, but we also know that there are others who hold to that vision: Christians of all faiths, black and white alike. Together we work for our common goals.

We are fully aware that there are vast numbers of Christians who are people of goodwill, for whom "Jew" has no derogatory implication. Large numbers of Jews and Christians have close and friendly personal relations that are as authentic as all true friendships should be. Unhappily, personal friendships exist side by side with another facet of our lives, our thought, in which "Christian" and "Jew" are abstractions—they are "the Christian," and "the Jew." It is those abstractions that retain the old stereotyped characteristics. Knowing people as individuals weakens hostilities and suspicions but, regrettably, it does not necessarily change the larger picture.

"Regrettably," for we Jews still have reservations as to the extent to which we can rely upon the goodwill, outreach, and supportive help of the Christian world.

How can we feel otherwise? The wounds of the Holocaust have not healed. The time has not yet come when the sheer weight of evidence tells us that it is time to abandon our concern. We are too close to the Holocaust when the Demon of Death wore a swastika but spoke more languages than German. We are still too close to the day when the nations at war with Germany declined to bomb and destroy the death camps or their feeder railroad tracks. We are still too close to the day of the international conference at Evian, where no nation offered to take into its land significant numbers of refugees who could still be saved.

How long will it take before it is no longer "too soon"? How long before we forget—and forgive?

Even though it is still too soon, even though we remember and shall always remember on *Yom HaShoa*, Holocaust Day, we Jews will not, on that account, lay down the tools to build a better world. We remember because the martyred dead should never be forgotten. But, remembering, we do not withdraw from the dialogue. The Holocaust is not the cause of our feeling of alienation. It is simply the most recent and the most horrendous demonstration of what is ultimately possible when a whole people is finally marked for destruction, after having been rejected for millennia.

No, we Jews shall not lay down the tools for bettering the human condition and therefore our own as well. There are some of us who do turn away from the dialogue because it is felt to be fruitless; they have no faith in its effectiveness. But by far the greater number of us favor continuing exchange—an exchange that has seen important alterations in official Christian theological positions, as well as significant alteration in church school teaching texts.

Reflecting upon ourselves as "the Jew in the world," remembering old hurts and recent violences, recalling the almost unbelievable pressures to which we have been subjected for so many centuries, it does seem astonishing that we Jews, when offering a toast, still find it possible to say, *"L'Chayyim"* (To Life!). But for us it is understandable. *"L'Chayyim"* is more than a toast; it is a manifesto—a manifesto of faith, faith in ourselves, faith in God, faith in our future, faith in the coming of the day when there will be acceptance of each by each, of all by all.

The World in the Jew

In the foregoing pages there has been described the Jew's understanding of what it means to be a Jew in terms of our response to the world in which we live. But there is more —much more. For there is not only the world in which we live; there is the world that lives in us.

To be a Jew is to have available a very special spiritual dimension of time and space. Our history was not just the story of what was described in the preceding pages on the Jew in the world; it is not merely made up of saddening experiences. Time past is also for us the ancient seedbed of festivals and holy days, of life-cycle rituals, of liturgy and worship. The awareness of those festivals and holy days, the experience of the life-cycle rituals, the articulation of liturgy and worship, carry with them a spiritual exhilaration, a deeply moving excitement that accompanies the sense of our foothold in the tenuous continuity of time. The consciousness that our prayers found their first statement millennia ago does not leave us untouched. Day by day, week by week, even though it be subtly, we converse with prophet and psalmist, and they speak to our innermost being.

When, each Passover, we sit at the seder, the ritual supper, even though we know that its actual format has changed over the centuries, the very words remind us that we are in touch with remote antiquity, that our celebration is only the most recent in a sequence that dates back to Bible times. The same sense of rootage in distant time past is present in our observance of the Festival of Booths, Sukkot. To hold in our hands the lulav and etrog, palm branch, myrtle, willow, and citron, is to keep us in touch with our beginnings. All our ritual celebrations are lines of communication with time gone by, given special strength because, whatever the reason for their observance, they are expressed through something we can hold, feel, taste, smell, see. How long since the first ram's horn was blown on the first day of Tishri, in keeping with the injunction to make of the day a day for the sounding of trumpets? Each year we hear it again, and we are immersed in the wellsprings of our origins.

This is something of the world in the Jew, a world wherein we have, as it were, one foot in all our yesterdays and one foot in today. We stand on two thresholds. It is an experience that is all the more welcome because in this generation there has been a widespread rejection of the past. The immediacy of communication has tended to erase the awareness of yesterday. Nations can rewrite their histories and make of their founders and principal actors nonpersons, expunging them from the records. Revulsion against recent excesses leads to the desire to be born anew. Time past is therefore regarded by many as best forgotten.

But, for us, time past is not only not rejected, it is the source of our spiritual strength. In the world in the Jew, there are to be found important elements of survival and meaning. The sense of time that we derive from calendar, life cycle, and worship is paralleled by that sense of time which comes with awareness of our continuation as faith and folk. The mystery or reality of mission, purpose, and covenant is sometimes debated and challenged today, sometimes hailed and probed with reverence. The ancient idea of covenant has been seriously threatened by the Holocaust. Where was God, it is asked, when the six million were slaughtered? What mission was fulfilled, what purpose answered? For some of us, the birth of the State of Israel, risen phoenixlike out of the ashes of these six million, seemed to be a reply to doubt and denial. So bound were we to the sense of covenant and purpose in our wanderings and misfortunes, so committed to the idea that it was all part of God's larger plan for us, that we could scarcely conceive of continuation without covenant as an impelling force.

Whatever the answer to the Holocaust, whatever the theological solutions to our dilemma, the sheer momentum of time carries us forward. While we move on, while we ponder on old Jacob, who merited the name Israel only after he had come away limping from his encounter with the divine, we search for newer ways in which our life as Jew can be molded; we probe new meanings and possibilities; new theologies are in the making.

Whatever the reason for our continued existence, that existence is a historic fact. We have been and we are. Throughout the past, there were many forces that made for adaptation and change. But in our persistence, we modeled ourselves on our ancestors in the wilderness, whose tribes encamped around the portable sanctuary, guarding its Stones of Witness. We, in turn, have protected Pentateuch and Prophets and the rest of our Scriptures, the very reading and study of which have kept us in touch with the sources of our faith.

In that inner world of the Jew, we have been richly nourished by the fruits of time, but we have also had to confront the spiritual cataclysms that threatened our very continuity as faith and folk. The winds blew hard, but our hands were always on the tiller, and, we hope, still are.

The sense of time, and of our place as faith and folk in its continuity, is to a lesser extent paralleled by our sense of extension in space. Actually, the word *sense* is better replaced by *awareness*, since we are speaking not about the shadowy people of remote time but about living contemporaries.

The most obvious evidence of our awareness of extension in space is manifested to us when, in our travels, it is virtually impossible not to find fellow Jews. There may be only a handful in some remote or rural community, or there may be larger populations in sizable world urban centers. Language, dress, custom, and even color may differ from our own, but we know them as our fellow Jews. They have shared the past with us; they share our present. They are the individualization of that generalized *we*. They may be among those who need the assistance of fellow Jews elsewhere; they may be those whose "lot has fallen in pleasanter places," but be they poverty-stricken or well-to-do, oppressed or free, they are all of them our alter egos, our equivalents in faith and folk. We are, each to the other, part of an extended family. When we worship together or break bread together, we are more than guests, we are kin.

Finally, there is another aspect of awareness, an aspect that has echoes of that emotion felt when we reached back into time. It comes to us when, celebrating those same festivals and holy days to which reference was made earlier, we realize that rituals and customs, prayers and practices are being carried out by our fellow Jews around the world, at virtually the same hour. Separated by space, we are joined by religious tradition and practice. It is an awareness that resonates an emotion deep within us. Historically, we often have been alienated and isolated in the world in which we live. But in the world within the Jew, we were—and are—never alone.

Despite the dangers and ravages of our time, despite the savage deaths of a third of our people, despite the threat that freedom itself has introduced into our religious and folk life, our greatest strength may well lie in the fact that on the graph of existence we are rooted in time and extended in space. This gives us the faith that we who were—and are—will still be.

Will we be the same as we are now? We do not and cannot know. Concepts may alter, forms of custom and worship may change, but of this we are certain—it is our manifesto to the world: *We shall be!*

EPILOGUE

Reflection on the inner and outer world of the Jew makes Jewish existence a continuing mystery in view of the enormous pressures to which we were subjected in both worlds. Comparable pressures exerted upon an individual would certainly have led to breakdown or perhaps even to suicide. At the very least they would have led to a neurotic inability to cope with everyday reality, with ordinary human relationships. Clearly, we must have had an almost indestructible inner strength; there must have been mechanisms at work to shore us up against the sledging of time.

Survival is in itself not too difficult. There is a momentum which carries peoples forward into their tomorrows, but are they the same people as when they began? What it comes down to is: How do the characteristics of the child manifest themselves in manhood and then in old age? What persists, what diminishes or is lost to sight? A people is not a person, but the question is valid. What have we taken with us from our beginnings? This book has offered a view of what may be called the externals of Jewish life—they are the articulation of the values that were, and are, of importance to us. In the preceding chapter I tried to tell something of what being Jewish means to the Jew. But there are deeper levels of existence, and it is these that call for the question.

Why we were from the beginning a fiercely independent folk, why we chose not to count ourselves among the nations, who can say? Our understanding of God, which grew from Genesis to Nathan to Amos to Hosea, and finally to the flowering genius of Isaiah, was the vision of spokesmen who could not make their peace with the mythic theologies of their day. They were what I think of as "conscientious rejectors," and as such represented the world view of our people as a whole. Someone has spoken of us as a tribal people with a universal outlook. But to be tribal does not mean to be primitive. It does mean to hold firmly to one's collective identity.

To hold firmly to one's collective identity makes survival possible only if there is some standard around which a people can rally under all conditions, something that articulates the values and convictions to which the Folk swears allegiance, as it were. That standard was, of course, Torah—Torah which included not only the Pentateuch but all Holy Writ and the subsequent second Torah of rabbinic interpretation. Christianity has long been fond of speaking of Judaism as a religion of law, whereas it, Christianity, is a religion of love. But rabbinic law, as Jacob Neusner has pointed out, has as its foundation a world view, which expresses itself through often necessarily detailed rules (*History of Religions*, vol. 16, no. 3, p. 235). Throughout the centuries of exile we willingly lived by those rules. They had created for us a home under whose roof we could not only survive but, more important, could find the rationale for survival.

The passion for independence, for the right to be what

we were, coupled with the kind of existence that reinforced us by giving us a nourishing way of life, kept us going despite the most adverse circumstances.

There were two radically important factors, which gave us the spiritual impetus to endure. The first was undoubtedly the sense of covenant. What befell us in our Exile, in our wanderings, was part of God's overall plan. To believe otherwise would have made life intolerable. It was the sort of faith that made it possible, in the face of disaster, to say "Gahm Zu LeTovah": even this is for the best.

Closely related to the feeling of covenant is the idea of messianism, which was such an important statement of our people's hope. Jewish messianism was profoundly revealing of our inner nature. One can see messianic speculation as the wish-fulfilling dream life of a people enduring generations of dispersion, hardship, rejection, and hostility. As such, it has always found a place in Jewish thought, since it was a deeply important aspect of our way of meeting life's disappointments and miseries.

What was the essence of such wish fulfillment? Was it the secretly held hope of turning the tables on our tormentors, a fantasy of revenge and punishment? To the contrary, the messianic dream, far from formulating suppressed or disguised plans for vindictive reprisal, was a vision of a world regenerated, a world of peace, brotherhood, justice, and security, such as the messianic vision of the prophets. The Exile inevitably underscored one facet of the prophetic vision: the restoration of the people of Israel to the land of Israel, the end of exile, a new life under God.

Now, to believe that the Exile is only temporary—even though "temporary" is stretched out over centuries—is to share in a "life lived in deferment," to use Gershom Scholem's apt expression. Living thus, anyone not knowing our people's history might imagine that we endured with a sort of depressed patience, our senses dulled. But the facts are otherwise. In an earlier chapter, I suggested that the adversities of our history were like a whetstone, against which our potential was honed to its keenest edge. Out of the deep wellsprings of our spiritual and intellectual resources, we managed to demonstrate a remarkable vitality. We not only learned to dig in and hold steady, but whenever given half a chance our best minds displayed the imaginative ability to make contributions to the cultural, economic, and scientific life of the day.

Throughout that life lived in deferment, no matter what the degree of opportunity to make such a contribution, the creative drive of gifted minds was not to be denied its outlet. The agelong tradition of study never came to an end. Deeply engrossed in the study of our own literature, we probed into its meaning, while we also read and studied the prevailing alien philosophies of the past and present. In short, there was ongoing intellectual ferment of one sort or another. Not all were scholars, philosophers, commentators, scientists, mathematicians, or physicians, but all did lend themselves to the proposition that the man of learning merited the highest status in the strata of social standing.

In the long run, as we have moved into modern times, other factors have played their role in our search for why we have endured. We have come to expect more from this self-conscious era. In an age when we speak of civil rights and human rights, it is inevitable that the passion for justice must be clearly articulated as also including justice for ourselves. The will to survive can be a manifesto to the world on the part of Moses' "stiff-necked people," a manifesto of which we Jews, collectively, are the text. The doctrine of covenant was badly mauled at Auschwitz; the

messianic return has, for most, been enacted in the creation of the State of Israel. Survival, going beyond socio-
religious values alone, is an act of determination to resist
to the end the singling out of the Jew as scapegoat for the
world's ills, for that singling out is itself the most acute of
those ills. Our fortunes and misfortunes are the measure of
the spiritual health or sickness of societies and nations.
That is our witness to the world.

We have endured because, despite the too often high
cost of maintaining our identity, the values inherent in our
always evolving religious civilization are adequate to our
spiritual and collective needs. The Jewish faith and folk
are, together, our ancestral home. We have been born in it
as have our forebears. It has weathered the elements; it has
occasionally been repaired or altered to accommodate new
generations. But its foundations are as solid as they were
at the beginning. It makes no sense to us to be told that we
would be more comfortable in someone else's home, or
that we should redesign our home in order to meet somebody's idea of what a house should be like.

This book has been a tour of that home. These closing
reflections have been an effort to explore with you why we
chose not to abandon it.

BIBLIOGRAPHY

The American Jewish Year Book. Philadelphia: American Jewish Committee and Jewish Publication Society of America.

Baron, Salo W. *The Jewish Community,* vol. 1, pp. 155–156. Philadelphia: Jewish Publication Society, 1942.

Ben-Gurion, David, ed. *The Jews in Their Land.* Garden City, N.Y.: Doubleday & Co., 1966.

Cohen, Arthur A. "The Holocaust and the Literary Imagination," *New York Times Book Review,* 18 January 1976, p. 19.

Donin, Hayim Halevy. *To Be a Jew,* chap. 6. New York: Basic Books, 1972.

The Ecumenist, vol. II, no. 1 (November/December 1972).

Gilbert, Martin. *Jewish History Atlas.* London: Weidenfeld and Nicolson, 1976.

Hereford, R. Travers. *Pharisaism,* pp. 68, 69. New York: Putnam & Sons, 1912.

Hertzberg, Arthur. *Introduction to the Zionist Idea,* p. 16. New York: Harper Torchbooks, 1966.

Kampf, Avram. *Contemporary Synagogue Art.* New York: Union of American Hebrew Congregations, 1966.

Marcus, Jacob R. *The Jew in the Medieval World,* pp. 28–32, 43. New York: Union of American Hebrew Congregations, 1938.

Maslow, Will. *The Structure and Functioning of the American Jewish Community.* New York: American Jewish Congress, 1974.

Millgram, Abraham. *Jewish Worship*, p. 411. Philadelphia: Jewish Publication Society, 1971.

Neusner, Jacob. *History of Religions*, vol. 16, no. 3 (February 1977), p. 235.

Rosten, Leo. *The Joys of Yiddish*. New York: McGraw-Hill, 1968.

Scholem, Gershom. *The Messianic Idea in Judaism*, p. 35. New York: Schocken Books, 1971.

Schweitzer, Albert. *History of the Jews Since the First Century A.D.*, p. 73. New York: Macmillan, 1971.

Trachtenberg, Joshua. *The Devil and the Jews*. New York: Harper Torchbooks, 1966.

INDEX